B-17
FLYING FORTRESS

L
337675
N
VE
L
237059
S
S

FLYING FORTRESS

H. P. Willmott

GALLERY BOOKS
An imprint of W.H. Smith Publishers Inc.
112 Madison Avenue
New York, New York 10016

A Bison Book

Published by Gallery Books
A Division if W H Smith Publishers Inc.
112 Madison Avenue
New York, New York 10016
USA.

Produced by Bison Books Corp.
17 Sherwood Place
Greenwich, CT 06830
USA

Printed in Hong Kong

1 2 3 4 5 6 7 8 9 10

ISBN 0-8317-0600-7

Page 1: **A B-17C in flight at an air show.**
Page 2-3: **With waist gunners and their formidable array of machine guns clearly visible, five B-17Gs of the 381st Bombardment Group (identified by an L on a black triangle, red facings) fly in a staggered Vee formation in the company of a lone P-51 Mustang fighter over southern England.**
Page 4-5: **A preserved B-17.**

CONTENTS

INTRODUCTION

'Ten-place, landplane monoplane, long-range high-altitude low-wing bomber.' The official description takes eleven words to define an aircraft that won international renown as the 'Flying Fortress.' It was a name that embraced many variants of an aircraft conceived eleven years before the end of World War II. The aircraft has many grounds for its claim to fame, but longevity of service is perhaps the most important. The Flying Fortress was certainly one of the very few aircraft that saw continuous service throughout the war despite having first flown as early as 1935. Admittedly the variants that were in service in 1945 – mostly B-17s of the F and G Marks – were significantly different from the first prototype and production models; throughout the war successive B-17s showed consistent improvements in both Marks and in-production Marks. However, at a time when the aviation industry was continuously pushing back the frontiers of knowledge with every year producing aircraft faster, more reliable and longer-ranged than the year before, the B-17 still managed to hold its own until the end of the war. By 1945 although still in production it was somewhat obsolescent, but that the aircraft saw continuous and unbroken service under war conditions speaks highly of an original design that allowed so much modification and change to be worked into the airframe. No other aircraft in World War II showed such adaptability and durability as the B-17.

A glowering pugnacious profile – machine guns snarling aggressively from a massive but not inelegant silhouette – helped the fame of the B-17. She was magnificently photogenic, especially when seen in formation. When alone against a brilliant azure sky or with her sisters, vapor trails marking their progress high above the clouds, the B-17 presents a superb subject for the camera. But the aircraft can also claim renown through the fact that the Mark G was built in greater numbers than any other single Mark of bomber. It is a record that is never likely to be broken. More B-24 Liberators than Fortresses were built, but no single Mark or variant could ever match the 8680-strong batch of B-17Gs built during the last two years of the war. Overall some 12,731 B-17s of all types were built, including prototypes and preproduction models. This total was easily exceeded by the Liberator, but this chunkier, more stolid aircraft could never match the grace of the Fortress or its claim to have been the first American bomber to enter the European Theater of Operations. Nor could it deny the Fortress the fact that the weight of the

Above: **In the foreground a Fortress III of the Royal Air Force in the company of a Fortress with USAAF markings. In fact both served with the RAF. The 19141 carries British camouflage and both British and American markings.**

USAAF's campaign of strategic bombing against Germany was carried by the B-17. The B-17 was the workhorse of the American air effort in Europe. Of the 47 Bombardment Groups that served with the 8th Air Force, the main American strategic bombing force in Europe, 29 were equipped wholly or mainly by the B-17. In carrying out the campaign of strategic bombing of Germany the Flying Fortress showed a tremendous resilience and ability to absorb punishment which frequently allowed it to make it home to base. That being said, however, it must be noted that nearly forty percent of all Fortresses built – over 5000 aircraft – failed to return from missions. It is perhaps inevitable that part of the fame of the aircraft must rest on the macabre fact that so many of the dead of the USAAF were lost when serving in the B-17.

Such are the bases for the claim to fame of the Boeing B-17 bomber, which it achieved despite the fact that it was not superior to many aircraft that enjoyed none of the limelight that came to the Fortress. The de Havilland Mosquito, for example, carried a bomb load not inferior to many B-17s; the B-24 was at least its equal and the Avro Lancaster could carry a bomb load three times the size of a normally-loaded Fortress. Such considerations are not of primary relevance and to argue the respective merits of one aircraft against another is seldom a worthwhile pastime, unless one happens to be an aircraft-manufacturer seeking a contract. Because of its strengths and despite its weaknesses the B-17 achieved lasting fame on account of a formidable fighting record in virtually every theater of war. Perhaps its record is only blemished by the tragedy that it shared with the whole of the American concept of strategic bombing. Because it failed to achieve all its objectives, the effectiveness of strategic bombing was doubted or neglected. Strategic bombing successfully distorted German production by diverting scarce resources from the critical fronts and ultimately achieved the ruination of the enemy's economy. The sad fact was, however, that strategic bombing could not achieve the single-handed defeat of the enemy as the more extreme of the prewar, air power enthusiasts had claimed. The simultaneous and total defeat of the enemy on land and at sea has tended to obscure the nature of the Allied strategic air victory and the tactical effect this had on the successful prosecution of the war on land.

H. P. Willmott

CONCEPTION

Above: The seemingly effortless grace and elegance of the B-17.
Below: The Fortress' sturdiness, strength and sense of rugged reliability is clearly portrayed. The massive redesign of fuselage and tailpiece, incorporated from the Mark E onward, added to the aura of power of the B-17.

The origins of the B-17 are confused because the whole of the career of the aircraft is linked intimately to the whole idea of strategic bombing. For the most part the roots of the B-17 are to be found in the dismal experience of World War I and the organizational arrangements of the American services in the interwar period. The indecisiveness of the war at sea and the prodigal useless sacrifice that characterized land battles between 1914 and 1918 led many men of different nationalities to consider the possibility – and indeed the desirability – of bringing about the defeat of an enemy by destroying his means of waging war. This involved the destruction of his means of production (and distribution) and the breaking of civilian willingness to sustain a war effort. This could be achieved by conducting a strategic air offensive aimed at the heartland of the enemy. This concept could only be successful if heavy bombers, in massive numbers and with massive payloads, could be concentrated for sustained operations.

Such an offensive was planned for 1919 by the British, the only combatant of World War I at that stage able to deploy a substantial long-range bomber force with heavier-than-air machines. In the event, given the state of German industry and morale in 1918, an offensive of this nature could not have proved anything of value, the war ending before the British had a chance to carry out their intentions. The idea of strategic bombing therefore remained untried and hence not disproved, making it very attractive to many people. But granted the fact that aviation was still relatively in its infancy the best and most earnest efforts of such men as Hugh Montague Trenchard in Britain, Giulio Douhet in Italy and William Mitchell in the USA not unnaturally failed to secure widespread acceptance for this radical notion of making war. For much of the interwar period the independent air forces of Britain and Italy encountered very great difficulty in preserving themselves as independent forces, clearly identifiable from the traditional services. Though successful in their rearguard actions, independent air forces remained the Cinderella of the services, with little money directed to them and with little stress placed upon the construction of bomber forces.

In the USA the ideas of strategic bombing, despite – and perhaps because of – the fiery efforts of Mitchell, failed to impress themselves upon a nation bent on isolation, cocooned by geographical remoteness from the fear of enemy attack and secure in its traditionalist reliance on the Navy – now American and not British – to safeguard national security. Accordingly, American aviation was divided between the Army and the Navy, the latter's interest naturally focusing on the revolutionary concept of the aircraft carrier. Within the Army all aircraft, reconnaissance planes, fighters and bombers became part of the Army Air Corps. The overriding idea of the AAC was tactical, not strategic. Its role was seen as providing support for ground forces over the battlefield, not carrying out a strategic offensive against an enemy homeland. But the nature of air warfare was such that the AAC was made a Major General's command and given a senior representative on the General Staff. The political post of Assistant Secretary of State for War, with special responsibilities for air matters, was created by the Coolidge administration with the approval of Congress.

In view of the flimsiness, unreliability, limited range and offensive power of aircraft before the 1930s, such an arrangement seems eminently sensible. But in the long term it was certain to be doomed as aircraft performance improved and the capacity of land-based aircraft grew more quickly than the power of carrier-borne aircraft. In 1931 recognition of this was given by an arrangement made between the Chief of the General Staff, General Douglas MacArthur, and the Chief of Naval Operations, Admiral Platt. By this arrangement the AAC was rescued from the obscurity to which it had been relegated and the financial parsimony to which it had been subjected by its being made responsible for all land-based air defense of the United States and her territories overseas. In order that the AAC could undertake this role an aircraft with a 200mph speed and a 2000lb bomb load was authorized. The more alert members of the AAC were not slow to appreciate that this arrangement and the aircraft involved presented possibilities for the development of a strategic air force with bombers to match. The Navy, on the other hand, was extremely slow to realize the full consequences of an action that permitted the AAC to usurp successfully part of the traditional, jealously guarded role of the Navy.

Nevertheless there were many problems of operating over the sea and attacking enemy shipping with which the AAC was totally unfamiliar at this time. These difficulties led to the creation in 1935 of a quite separate organization, General Headquarters Air Force (GHQAF), to supervise and co-ordinate all air action supposedly subordinate to the Navy in maintaining the seaward defenses of the United States. The Navy was growing increasingly concerned by the trend of events and after the long-range interception of an Italian ship by GHQAF aircraft, in 1938 secured the restriction of GHQAF activity to within 100 miles of the American coast. The Navy feared that its role would be taken over by the AAC and was anxious to emasculate GHQAF – the opportunity to achieve the latter presented itself with the incident involving

the Italian ship. By 1938, however, such a restriction was totally unrealistic. Either the Navy operated all coastal aircraft itself or the range restriction had to be abolished. It was only sensible to intercept an enemy at the greatest possible range. Perhaps the most significant fact about the new arrangement was that the whole incident was triggered off, and the subsequent row over the role of land-based aviation brought to a head, by three preproduction experimental aircraft designated the Y1B-17. These were the forerunners of the B-17. In the aftermath of the incident the head of GHQAF, Brigadier General Frank M Andrews, was removed from his post because of his staunch and continued advocacy of the concept of strategic bombing.

One of the earliest and clearest indications of the trend of events that were to show the impracticality of the 1931 arrangement – which confirmed the Navy's hesitations regarding the role of land-based aircraft – came in 1934 when ten B-10 Martin bombers of the AAC flew nonstop from Alaska to Seattle. These bombers were steel-framed, twin-engined monoplanes, and their single action really highlighted the question of whether it was wise to trust in a concept of continental defense that was based on slow surface ships. Even with carriers the Navy had no comparable ability, yet in 1934 the AAC invited tenders for an aircraft whose specifications demanded an ability to make a direct flight from the United States to Alaska, Panama or Hawaii. To a 5000-mile range were added demands for a speed of 200mph and a payload of 2000lb.

Previous to this the Boeing Aircraft Company had produced a series of aircraft, mostly transports, that had made the company pioneers in the field of long-range aircraft with a good freight-carrying capacity. With the Model 247 transport Boeing had secured a considerable lead over all its rivals, but even Boeing hesitated when the specifications of the new aircraft demanded by the AAC were appreciated. The specifications were extremely exacting, but Boeing began to draw

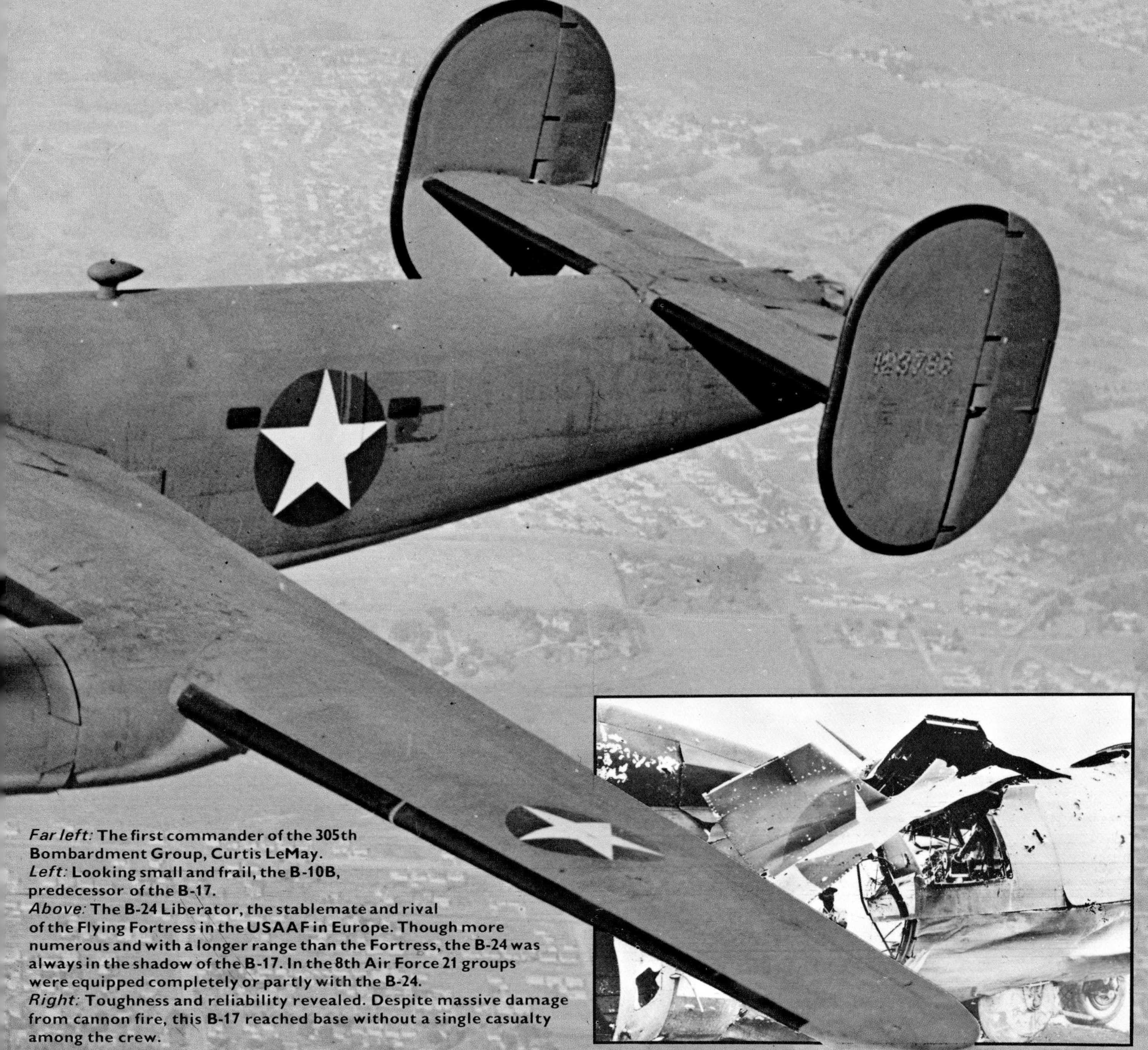

Far left: The first commander of the 305th Bombardment Group, Curtis LeMay.
Left: Looking small and frail, the B-10B, predecessor of the B-17.
Above: The B-24 Liberator, the stablemate and rival of the Flying Fortress in the USAAF in Europe. Though more numerous and with a longer range than the Fortress, the B-24 was always in the shadow of the B-17. In the 8th Air Force 21 groups were equipped completely or partly with the B-24.
Right: Toughness and reliability revealed. Despite massive damage from cannon fire, this B-17 reached base without a single casualty among the crew.

up plans for such an aircraft. Hardly had work begun on what Boeing designated the Model 294 when the AAC requested submissions for a replacement for the B-10. The Boeing firm thus faced a very delicate choice. It risked falling between two stools if it tried to compete for both contracts. It knew that if it failed to secure orders then there was no possibility of financial remuneration from the government for the work that had been done. On the other hand Boeing was well aware of the fact that follow-up contracts could prove extremely profitable.

By the time Boeing formally decided to enter the race for the new multi-engined bomber to replace the B-10 at its Board of Directors' meeting on 26 September 1934, preliminary planning and development work had been in hand for some time. The first piece of metal cutting took place in August, some six weeks before the Board decided to risk $270,000 of the company's money in the venture. The work that had been done on the Model 294 – which flew on 18 October 1937 as the XBLR-1 – had served to convince Boeing that the new bomber on which they were working, called the Model 299, had to amalgamate the best features of the 247 and 294. This involved giving the Model 299 four engines. In making this choice Boeing opted for a design that radically differed from those being submitted by its only serious rivals, Martin and Douglas, both of whom were relying on the conventional two-engined version for their designs.

On 16 July 1935, just eleven months to the day when the first part of the aircraft had been built, the Boeing competitor for the most lucrative contract offered the American aviation industry since the end of World War I was rolled out of her hangar on Boeing Field, Seattle. By contemporary standards she was enormous, and the impression she created was equally large. Weighing some 21,600lb empty and provided – but not armed – with numerous machine-gun positions, she was immediately (but mathematically incorrectly) dubbed, 'The Fifteen-Ton Flying Fortress.' The name, of course, stuck, but the weight was to be greatly exceeded in time by the later variants of this aircraft. The sheer impact of Model 299, on production redesignated X-13372, can be gauged by a direct comparison with the B-10 bomber she was intended to replace. The B-10, carrying a four or five-man crew in an aircraft whose span was 70ft 6in and whose length was 44ft 8in, was less than half the weight of the X-13372. Her twin engines gave her a top speed of 210mph and she had a range of about 700 miles with a 1000lb load. With extra fuel the range of the B-10 could be extended to about 1200 miles. The X-13372, on the other hand, measured 103ft 9in by 61ft 10in and could carry a crew of eight, four of whom would be machine gunners. Her tests revealed her to possess a maximum speed of 236mph at 10,000ft and a service ceiling of 24,600ft. Her maximum range was 3000 miles, some 600 miles beyond what was considered to be her normal operating range, and she was capable of carrying a load four times that carried by the Martin. In every respect the X-13372 had exceeded all the requirements made of her by more than considerable margins. In April 1934 the AAC had demanded an aircraft with a 2000-mile range, a payload of 2000lb and a top speed of 220mph at 10,000ft. It was not for nothing that one of the first AAC officers to see her was heard to comment that the X-13372 was an airborne battle cruiser.

The power, speed, punch and range of a battle cruiser were present indeed in the X-13372, but she also shared the battle cruiser's graceful lines and awesome beauty. She had superbly clear rounded lines that gave her an easy elegance enabling what was a very large tailpiece to rest on the top of a wide wing area and circular sectionalized fuselage with unassuming indifference. To add to the streamlined effect, the undercarriage was retractable. This again set her apart from the B-10 and most other military aircraft of the time. By every possible standard in the X-13372 Boeing had produced an extremely advanced and formidable aircraft, well ahead of its time and of any competitor for the AAC order. Confidence in the Boeing camp must have been very high when the X-13372, under the control of the firm's chief test pilot, Leslie R Towers, took to the air for the first time shortly before dawn on 28 July 1935.

The maiden flight went well. Like all her successors the X-13372 proved an extremely easy aircraft to fly. She handled easily, though she was subject to some wing turbulence, but she was stable and quick to respond to the controls. Her first

Above: **Boeing's first experiment with a heavy bomber, the XBLR-1. It first flew in 1937 as the XB-15 and saw service as the XC-105 as a cargo and personnel transport. Length 87ft 7in, Span 149ft, Weight 70,706lb, Range 5130, Speed 200 mph.**
Below: **The B-18, the rival to the X-13372.**

Above and left: **The YB-17, later renumbered the Y1B-17. The group photograph shows a formation of Fortresses in service with 2nd Bombardment Group, GHQAF. It was as part of this unit that much of the pioneering work with the B-17 was done, the aircraft breaking many speed records without loss.**

flight and the subsequent series of ground and air tests to which she was subjected by Boeing (before going to the AAC) all proved eminently satisfactory and at 0345 hours on 20 August with Towers again at the controls, she rose to the skies for what was to be her toughest test to date. She was setting out for the AAC evaluation center at Wright Field, Dayton, Ohio, in an effort to convince the airmen that this was the aircraft they needed. On her way to Dayton, before the AAC tests had even started, the X-13372 achieved a remarkable piece of 'one-upmanship' that gave her a decided edge over her rivals. She arrived at about 1700 hours, having covered the 2100-mile journey in nine hours at an average speed of 232mph. This made the would-be Boeing bomber faster than any front-line fighter in American service at that time, a point of satisfaction to all at Boeing but of no small concern to the AAC and the service chiefs. In her subsequent trials the aircraft proved more than equal to any task set her and far superior to her rivals, but on 30 October during a routine test, with Towers and Major Peter P Hill at the controls, the X-13372 stalled and crashed on takeoff. The aircraft was burned out and both Towers and Hill died as a result of the burns they had sustained. In this accident neither pilot error nor mechanical failure had played a part. Because of its massive tail, the X-13372 had been fitted with a spring locking device to prevent damage to the flaps and rudder being caused by the wind while the aircraft was on the ground. This lock had not been removed prior to takeoff.

Nevertheless, despite the fact that the X-13372 was not in any way responsible for its own loss, it was not unnatural that the accident should have dampened enthusiasm for such an advanced aircraft. Critically, Boeing had no second aircraft with which to complete the AACs series of tests, and this left the way open for Boeing's only serious rival, the Douglas B-18, to secure the order for 133 aircraft. It cannot be doubted that the accident had cost Boeing the chance to bring home this production contract but it must be said that Boeing, in some ways, had hardly helped its own cause by producing in the X-13372 such an advanced aircraft. At over $260,000 per aircraft, the Boeing submission was more than three times more expensive than the B-18. This was a very important consideration at a time when the services were conscious of the need to get value for money. The price of high sophistication, as manifest in the X-13372, was high, and when this went hand in hand with an aircraft that crashed during trials (irrespective of reason), the likelihood of a favorable contract being secured was rather slim. But the AAC, despite giving out the contract to Douglas, had been sufficiently impressed by the X-13372 to give an order for thirteen preproduction models and a fourteenth airframe in order to carry on evaluation trials. This order was given on 17 January 1936. The thirteen aircraft were designated YB-17. This was amended in November to Y1B-17 in order to indicate the funding arrangement of the aircraft.

Just as the initial development of the X-13372 had taken eleven months, so the development and production of the Y1B-17 took the same time. Appropriately, in view of the fact that 1936 was an Olympic year – the Games ironically being held in Berlin – the motto of the new batch of aircraft might well have been, 'Faster, Higher, Stronger.' The Y1B-17 showed that Boeing had not rested on its laurels but had used the time since the first prototype to make many improvements with the new batch of aircraft. By being nearly 7ft longer and a ton heavier than the X-13372, the Y1B-17 had room for one more crew member and had rearranged the flight deck in order to place the pilot and the copilot alongside one another. This was common in civil aircraft; it was not normal in military aircraft at this time. Undercarriage and armament improvements had been worked into the new aircraft, but the most striking features of the Y1B-17 were its enhanced speed, endurance and lift capability. In the place of the X-13372s four Pratt and Whitney Hornet R-1690-E nine-cylinder radial air-cooled engines, each capable of 750hp, were four 930hp Wright Cyclone GR-1820-39 (G2) engines. These gave the slightly heavier aircraft a top speed of 256mph at 14,000ft. With an extreme range of 3400 miles – an improvement of 400 miles – the Y1B-17 had a service ceiling of 30,000ft. Like the X-13372 the Y1B-17 had a normal bomb load of 4000lb; this could be doubled though only at the cost of considerably reducing her operational range.

Undoubtedly some aeronautical geniuses must have been present at the birth of the B-17. However, on 7 December 1936, just five days after the first flight of a Y1B-17, the first of the new aircraft nose-dived on landing as a result of the brakes seizing. Despite this inauspicious start – which prompted a congressional inquiry – the Y1B-17 subsequently prospered. The first was delivered to the AAC in January 1937. Subsequently as they were produced and delivered from Boeing the AAC retained a single aircraft at Wright Field for experimental work and detailed the remaining eleven to join a new organization, the 2nd Bombardment Group, GHQAF.

GHQAF and 2nd BG on the one hand and the Y1B-17 on the other hand might well have been made for each other. Despite its official role GHQAF, under the direction of Andrews, was primarily interested in strategic bombing; GHQAF wanted to test the concept. GHQAF had to build up the concept and the force needed from base roots because there was no fund of knowledge on which to draw and GHQAF had no real idea of what was involved, either organizationally or operationally. It did not know, and there was no means of knowing, what could and could not be expected from aircraft, and there was no certainty that the Y1B-17 might provide some of the answers or be the answer itself. GHQAF was basically groping in the dark. It wanted to deploy two groups, one on the Pacific coast and the other on the Atlantic. In this manner the primary function of GHQAF – the sorting out of problems involved in the provision of air power over the sea against an enemy invasion force – could be discharged, but for the moment the 2nd BG, with its experimental Y1B-17s, had to suffice. But in this aircraft, all service models of which were fully concentrated with the group by August 1937, GHQAF found that it had an aircraft that could be realistically tested, albeit under peacetime conditions, as a bomber.

The results of the tests to which the Y1B-17 was subjected by GHQAF were astounding. The 2nd BG registered nearly 10,000 flying-hours and almost 2,000,000 miles in all-weather flying without a single accident. Its flights took it over all parts of the USA in the course of which the Y1B-17 broke the existing east-west and west-east records with ease (12 hours 50 minutes and 10 hours 46 minutes respectively). In February 1938 in a goodwill gesture for the inauguration of the new president in Argentina the Group flew from Miami to Buenos Aires, staging through Lima in Peru. The 5036-mile flight was covered in less than 27 hours in the air. It was an impressive performance that showed the intercontinental capability of the aircraft. Everything that the Y1B-17 was asked to do she did superlatively – including the interception of the Italian ship that sparked off the row between the US Navy and GHQAF and cost Andrews his job, GHQAF the role to which it aspired and the Y1B-17 its future – or so it appeared at the time.

Two sets of circumstances were to save Andrews, GHQAF and the Y1B-17. The first was the remarkable Y1B-17 itself. In

the spring of 1938, a fully-laden Y1B-17, packed with instruments to collect data on performance, was flying in low overcast conditions over its base at Langley Field when it encountered exceptionally rough air. The aircraft, piloted by Lieutenant William Bentley, was thrown into a stall and into no less than nine spins before Bentley was able to regain control of his aircraft and bring it safely in to land. The result of this unpremeditated event was to make the AAC look a second time at the aircraft it had on its hands. By any standard the wings of the aircraft should have been ripped off as a result of forces the aircraft had never been designed to resist. The instruments aboard and subsequent calculations showed that the aircraft had indeed withstood stress far greater than that allowed for by the designers. Rivets had popped and the wings had been bent as a result of these unanticipated acrobatics, but the aircraft had survived and was able to be repaired. The AAC was quick to take the lesson. The airframe that had been ordered for ground tests on the stress level that could be absorbed by the aircraft was immediately fitted out as an aircraft. Redesignated Y1B-17A (Number 37369), it flew for the first time on 29 April 1939.

This aircraft in its turn proved to be as much an advance over the Y1B-17 as that aircraft had been over the X-13372. What set the Y1B-17A apart from her stable companions were four Moss–General Electric turbo-superchargers fitted to the tops of her new 1000hp Cyclone G-1820-51 (G5) engines while the fairings over the nacelles were removed. These engines and the superchargers made the Y1B-17A nearly 50mph faster than the Y1B-17, allowing her to break the magical 300mph figure for the first time. Her effective maximum speed, however, was 295mph at 25,000ft. She had a service ceiling of 38,000ft and a range of 3600 miles. In one test she was to set a record that by aviation standards was to last a long time. She lifted an 11,000lb bomb load over a distance of 620 miles at an average speed of 233mph. Under normal circumstances she could carry a 4000lb payload, but for operational purposes it was envisaged that she would carry a 2500lb bomb load over 1500 miles. With the Y1B-17A the AAC really had a strategic bomber of unrivaled power, indeed an aircraft worthy of her name. It was with considerable gratitude that the AAC formally took possession of the aircraft on 31 January 1939.

The timing of the delivery could hardly have been better for the cause of strategic bombing because by this stage the second of the two factors was being called into play. The natural march of events was beginning to move in favor of the idea of strategic bombing and the heavy bomber concept.

Above: **The airframe that was developed into a unique aircraft, the YB-17A, later the Y1B-17A and B-17A. The first heavy bomber with superchargers.**

Certainly the massive improvement in aircraft performance had been a major factor in making many see the idea of strategic bombing in a new light. But what had really begun to break down opposition to the bomber and strategic bombing in the American political and military hierarchy had been the abject capitulation of the British and French in the face of German threats at Munich in September 1938. The US administration realized only too well that Anglo-French spinelessness in large part derived from their consciousness of their inferiority to the Luftwaffe. That the power of the German Air Force had been greatly exaggerated by a grossly inflated figure was of little account. The British and French had been haunted by the prospect of their cities being razed if they attempted to go to the aid of Czechoslovakia.

The administration was also aware of the trend of events in the western Pacific where the Japanese were building up their armaments at the greatest possible speed while being involved in a lurid and violent conquest of China. Nanking in China and Guernica in Spain, both cities being devastated by virtually unopposed bomber forces, were examples that no American administration could afford to ignore. It was not that the USA itself felt threatened, but Washington was beginning to consider seriously the deterrent effect that possession of major strategic bombing forces might have on would-be aggressors. Neither the administration nor the electorate wanted war or sought any change in the isolationist policies that had been pursued since the days of Woodrow Wilson, but by 1939 the purse strings were beginning to be loosened and much of the service resistance to the idea of strategic bombing was beginning to ebb. It was at this time that the Liberator, the aircraft that was to share with the Fortress the task of strategic bombing in the ETO, was ordered. With the trials and evaluation of the Y1B-17 and Y1B-17A complete, these aircraft were redesignated the B-17 and B-17A respectively while orders were given for 39 production models, designated the B-17B. The first of these new aircraft took to the air on 27 June 1939 and all 39 were to be delivered into commission between July 1939 and March 1940. They were not to know that they were to be followed in the next five years by a further 12,677 Fortresses and five main Marks which were to operate in many services of different nations and in many and varied theaters of war.

DEVELOPMENT–B, C

With the B-17/B-17A the AAC had an aircraft that seemed capable of carrying out the role of a strategic bomber. Technically this was true, for the aircraft was reliable, fast and well armed. But the concept of bombing to which the AAC was committed was daylight operations against precision targets by heavy bombers that relied on high speed and strong defensive firepower to resist fighter interceptors. Time and events were to show that such hopes were to be highly exaggerated, but in the period 1939–41 the AAC never fully appreciated the difficulties inherent in bombing operations. It was aware that advanced though the X-13372, Y1B-17 and Y1B-17A had been when first they flew, further development and modification would be needed for the B-17 concept to operate effectively. The process of continuous change between Marks and production of individual Marks was therefore very rapid with three improved versions of the B-17/B-17A appearing in an evolutionary procession in 1940 and 1941. Thereafter the various changes, first embodied in the B-17E, were more fundamental and revolutionary in character.

Seemingly the B-17B was very similar to the B-17/B-17A. As the first batch of aircraft specifically ordered by the AAC to fulfill an operational role, the B-17B in fact showed many small but very significant changes from its predecessors though its overall performance was very little different from that of the B-17A. The most obvious changes were the altered settings for the turbo-superchargers and a considerable improvement in the nose arrangements to give both cleaner lines and more space to the navigator and bomb-aimer. The cost of this was the removal of the nose blister, the original transparent cone with a bubble-mounted machine gun being discarded in favor of a new Plexiglas fairing. In place of the ventral cutout below the nose where the bomb-aiming panel had been located in the B-17A, the B-17B carried a flat on which was mounted the celebrated Norden gyro stabilized bombsight. (Subsequently this bombsight, which was claimed to be highly accurate at an altitude of 30,000ft, was to be linked to the autopilot by means of automatic flight control equipment. The first occasion on which this arrangement was used operationally was on 18 March 1943.) The rudder and flaps of the B-17B were enlarged in order to improve the handling characteristics of the aircraft while a hydraulic braking system replaced the pneumatic type employed on previous Marks.

Above: **After extensive modification the B-17C entered service as the Fortress I with the Royal Air Force, but its combat record was not very impressive.**

Even while the production of the B-17B was in hand orders were given out for a further 38 aircraft of a new improved type. This was the B-17C, the first flight of which took place on 21 July 1940. This was a matter of a mere seven weeks after the operational deployment of all the completed B-17Bs and even before the new B-17C first flew a further order for another 42 improved aircraft, the B-17D, had been issued. The increasing tempo of orders and the qualitative and quantitative improvements in the AACs demands all served to emphasize the

D D MARKS

Above: **One of the new B-17Cs enters service with the US Army Air Corps on 29 July 1940. Even before it flew, orders for a new Mark had been given.**

growing concern felt by the administration over events in Europe. These orders also had one other effect; they paved the way for the much larger B-17E construction program.

The most striking feature of the B-17C was its increased weight (fully loaded it was nearly 50,000lb) and a greatly improved performance, largely brought about by another major engine improvement. Boosted 1200hp Wright Cyclone GR-1820-65 (G-205A) engines, with turbo-superchargers below the engines, gave the B-17C a top speed of 323mph at 25,000ft though she had a slower rate of climb at takeoff than the B-17B. The higher performance of the Mark C also owed something to improved aerodynamics. The waist-gun blisters were removed in favor of flat gun panel windows which were shifted slightly rearward in order to give the waist gunners better fields of vision and arcs of fire. The dorsal gun position was similarly treated, all three gun positions having to shed their protective windows when entering combat. The ventral gun position was also redesigned to form a smooth 'bathtub' which though longer and larger than previous ventral fittings was more harmonious and graceful than previous ventral arrangements. The nose gun was removed and replaced by two separate guns mounted inside the nose cone but angled through each side of the fuselage. To complete the armament changes both ventral and dorsal positions were given twin 0.5in Browning machine guns.

With the B-17D Boeing made minor though important alterations to the basic B-17C. The new aircraft could be outwardly distinguished from the Mark C only by its redesigned engine cowlings and cooling shutters which were incorporated in an effort to overcome problems caused by engines overheating as a result of their prolonged climbs to operational altitude. Internally, however, the changes were more significant. Boeing revised the electrical circuits of the Fortress and with the Mark D introduced self-sealing fuel tanks and improved armor protection for the crew. Subsequently many of the B-17Cs were recalled and subjected to conversions in order that they incorporate many of these improvements.

Below: **One of the first B-17Ds. This version showed many small advances over the Mark C, but was the last before a major redesign of the airframe.**

WAR AND THE B-17E

The B-17Ds were the last of the original B-17s. Up until that Mark all Flying Fortresses had exhibited certain basic characteristics: smallness of numbers built, minor alterations of silhouette and small (or relatively small) changes in internal arrangements, armaments and specialist pieces of equipment. The cumulative effect of all these measures was by no means negligible, but with the B-17D the qualitative improvements were beginning to level out; the aircraft in the form it had attained was really incapable of much more development. If the B-17 was to undergo any further improvements then they could only be achieved by a revolutionary recasting of certain design features that had to be concentrated upon modification to the airframe.

Normally the impetus toward revolutionary redesign of a weapon or piece of equipment stems from the experience of combat. In part certain of the changes worked into the B-17D resulted from such a source, but one of the remarkable features in the history of the development of the B-17 is that while the B-17E differed in so many ways from her earlier sisters as to be revolutionary – indeed almost another aircraft – the changes were in large part not dictated by combat evaluation but by Boeing's anticipation of criticism and advice. In fact the first of the B-17Es flew on 5 September 1941 – three months before the enforced entry of the USA into the war. By the time war came the production lines were fully engaged in building an aircraft that was largely immune from the weaknesses of earlier Marks, at that time being ruthlessly exposed by the Japanese Zero-sen fighter. It was ironic, in a way, that the sacrifice of the B-17Bs, Cs and Ds in the opening months of the Pacific War did not result in major redesign features; the changes had already been put into effect before the outbreak of war. Such was Boeing's flair and ingenuity in being able to anticipate problems.

The B-17 saw combat even before the Americans entered the war, but that combat experience came too late to affect the B-17E. In March 1940 the British purchasing mission in Washington obtained the permission of the Roosevelt administration to secure the first twenty B-17Cs to come off the assembly lines. The purchase was covered by the open deception that these aircraft were to be used for training duties only by the Royal Air Force, but in fact it was understood that the British would make their combat analysis available to the Americans. In view of the fact that in September 1939 the USA only had 23 operational Fortresses and only 53 were delivered in 1940, the American decision, though not disinterested, was extremely generous and all that could be reasonably expected at the time.

The twenty B-17Cs – and, secretly, their crews and ground maintenance parties – were taken over by the RAF and allocated to No 90 Squadron at West Raynham, Norfolk. The force was concentrated only as late as May 1941, partly because the British insisted upon certain major changes being worked into (what they called) the Fortress I before they accepted delivery of the aircraft and committed it to combat.

Above: One of the first Flying Fortresses to enter active service. A Mark C in service with the RAF as the Fortress I.
Below: This Boeing B-17E was specially rebuilt for General Douglas MacArthur as his flying staff headquarters. It was named 'Bataan' and ferried MacArthur throughout Southeast Asia.

The awesome power of US industry:
1 and 3. Main body assembly line at the Boeing factories in Seattle.
2. The Vega plant at Burbank.
4. The Boeing assembly line for the tailpiece. Note the massiveness of the tailpiece and (absent) rudder, compared to the smallness of the rear fuselage, and the employment of women on production line.
5. Inboard wing section showing engines and fuel tank caps. Outboard wing sections were made separately.

4

5

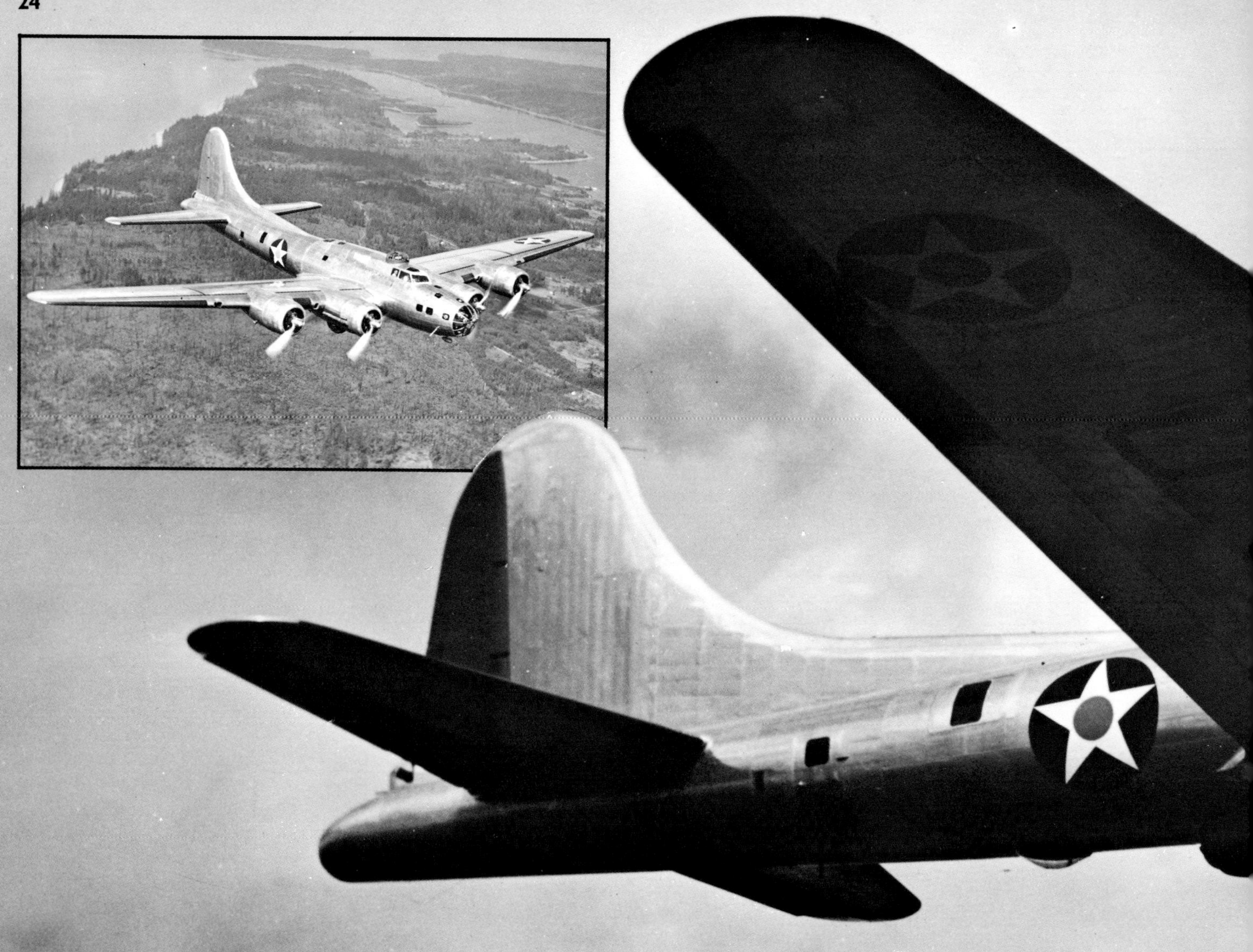

Among the changes about which the British were adamant were the installation of self-sealing tanks and a heavier forward armament. These changes the British considered essential if the aircraft was to have any chance of survival in the hard school of combat over Germany. The RAF had gone to war in 1939 with much the same ideas as the AAC regarding the desirability and practicability of daylight bombing. By 1941 experience had convinced the RAF that not merely were there drawbacks to such a plan of campaign, but that it was prohibitively expensive. The British losses in daylight raids over Germany from the start of the war were crippling to the extent that area bombing of industrial areas at night had been substituted as the only means of carrying out a strategic bombing offensive. Thanks to their own combat experience over Germany and the German defeat in the Battle of Britain in 1940, the British drew the correct conclusion that daylight bombing could not be successful because the bombers, lacking the protection of long-range fighters, could not defend themselves. The British were skeptical of the claims made by the AAC (renamed the US Army Air Force after 20 June 1941) on behalf of the Flying Fortress. The British doubted the ability of the B-17C to fight its way to a target and there was a distinct coolness toward an aircraft that was so big and costly in terms of scarce manpower resources but which possessed so little punch. The American faith in their ability to fight their way to and from a target in formation and en masse was unshaken by British doubts and warnings, and the RAF did not endear itself to the USAAF by its tactical employment of the Fortress I. It was almost as if the RAF raids with the B-17Cs were deliberately staged to show up the aircraft's limitations rather than its strengths. In RAF hands in 1941 the B-17C showed itself capable of absorbing massive battle damage and still making it home safely at 30,000ft, but very little else. The British used their Fortress Is in very small groups against targets that tended to be very well defended. The resultant losses were heavy and with accidents accounting for several other aircraft, the few survivors were sent either to North Africa (and two to India where incredibly they rejoined a USAAF formation) or to Coastal Command. At this stage in the war for the RAF to assign anything at all to Coastal Command was tantamount to its being condemned as unfit for further service.

The British view of the Fortress was rather damning, but there was justification for many of the criticisms made by the British. The B-17C did tend to shudder at bomb release and was not a good bombing platform. She was vulnerable to head-on fire and attacks from the rear and from below. The Fortress's lack of protection and self-sealing tanks were serious matters, and the speed with which Boeing acted on this indicates the validity of the British criticism. The Americans, on the other hand, were correct in their criticism of British tactics and the evident lack of faith in the aircraft shown by the

Left, right and below: **The B-17E, the last of the Marks produced solely by Boeing before Vega and Douglas entered production. The Mark E showed massive improvements over earlier versions, most notably in stronger defensive armament and stability as a bombing platform. The change in the ventral gun position after the 112th production model is clearly shown in the photographs.**

RAF, but they were far too sanguine in their belief that 'the bomber will always get through.' Experience was to show that the Americans asked far too much of the Fortress; even at its peak the Fortress could not withstand concerted fighter attacks and had only a short life expectancy in skies controlled by enemy fighters.

In fact both the Americans and the British were wrong in their views of strategic bombing. The Americans saw strategic bombing as a means of securing air supremacy; they failed to see that air supremacy had to be achieved before a bombing offensive could be successful. The British, conscious from the start of the war of the bomber's vulnerability, attempted to evade the real issue by seeking the cover of darkness in order to bomb while avoiding heavy losses. In 1941 British night bombing was against specific targets; in 1942 it shifted to general area attacks when it was realized that the degree of accuracy needed for night precision bombing was not possible with the equipment then available. The fact of the matter was that American and British fighters had to oppose German fighters over their own cities before the bombing attacks could begin to inflict significant damage without having to suffer unendurable losses. At this stage of the war, the USAAF was confusing various issues while the RAF was intent on evading them. In 1941, however, without any trace of national bias, it is probably fair and accurate to state that the B-17, while a fine aircraft, was not a good bomber, and that at the very best the case for it was nonproven. Its combat record can be described as indifferent.

Many of the technical criticisms of the B-17C had been anticipated by Boeing and were being remedied in the new order of B-17Es. This aircraft proved to be extremely significant in the development and history of the B-17 on purely technical grounds, as well as on two other grounds. Firstly, it was ordered in unprecedented numbers. To a world numbed by the sheer scale of American output in the course of World War II, an order for 512 aircraft might not seem very much, but in pre-Pearl Harbor days this was a massive order. It must be remembered, moreover, that at the time the order was placed only 119 earlier variants had been built or were being built. What was really important about the order was the fact that it was based more on an act of faith and hope than solid judgment on the part of the Army Air Force.

Secondly, in order to build aircraft in such numbers the USAAF was led to demand a complete reorganization of production. Exclusive manufacture of the Flying Fortress was taken out of the hands of Boeing and placed in the hands of a consortium of Boeing, Douglas and Vega. The Boeing factory at Seattle was augmented by another plant built at Wichita, Kansas, while Douglas, the long-standing rival of Boeing, found itself opening a factory at Long Island, California, in order to build an aircraft to take over from the B-17. This pooling of resources was supposed to take effect with the

Mark E production order, but in fact the Douglas and Vega companies both encountered such teething problems – inevitable in setting up complex assembly lines – that the B-17E order was the last to be exclusively completed by Boeing. Only in the long term was the USAAF's arrangement to show its true worth because this pooling of resources did for Flying Fortress production what Henry Kaiser did for Liberty Ship construction.

The combining of the three companies plus the expansion of factory space and production lines left the Americans in a position subsequently to step up production to a level that no other nation could possibly have envisaged, still less matched. The significance of the measure can be seen by the fact that the first B-17F left the production line on 30 May 1942; by the time production on that particular Mark ceased some fifteen months later, 3405 had been built. Of these Douglas and Vega had contributed 605 and 500 respectively. Thereafter production shifted to the B-17G and of the 8680 produced before the order books were closed in April 1945 Vega produced 2250 and Douglas 2395. Between them, therefore, the two secondary companies built nearly 48 percent of all the B-17Fs and B-17Gs constructed. At their peak in March 1944 the three companies between them were producing 130 B-17Gs a week, or twice the weekly loss rate in the ETO. It was about this time that Boeing's Seattle plant touched its record production level of sixteen complete B-17Gs a day. To properly gauge the significance of these figures of overall production in general and that of Vega and Douglas in particular, it is worth noting that between them Douglas and Vega covered what is euphemistically termed wastage. About 5000 B-17s were lost from all causes during the war, most of them naturally in the last two years of the war in Europe. Douglas and Vega made good these losses. Though this part of the story is not directly relevant to discussion of the B-17E, it must always be remembered that the massive expansion of construction and the numbers of B-17Fs and B-17Gs available to the Americans in 1944–45 were only possible as a result of certain actions taken while the B-17D was being built and before the order for the B-17E was finalized.

In September 1941, when the first of the B-17Es took to the skies, such matters remained in the distant future. For the moment the new Mark held all attention because she represented a definitive break with earlier B-17s. The most striking feature of the Mark E was her totally altered profile. In the place of the long but relatively thin fuselage and huge tailpiece – a phenomenon that led to her being called 'the big-assed bird' – there appeared a much longer aircraft, 73ft 10in in length, with a greatly enlarged rear fuselage. This allowed the already big empennage to be increased still further in order to improve the aircraft's stability at extreme altitude and during bomb release. The increase was incorporated into a massive dorsal fin that stretched forward down the airframe until it was almost on the upper level with the wings. By itself this constituted a thirty percent design alteration of the aircraft. Gone were the long fine lines and seemingly disproportionately large tailpiece; in their places was an alteration that made for a fuller aircraft, by its very appearance more menacing, tenacious and powerful. But even with this dorsal fin the

B-17E retained much of the aesthetic grace of earlier marks. In addition, the alterations provided for a sting in the end of the tail. The wider, stronger fuselage permitted for the first time the location of a manually-powered turret, armed with twin 0.5in Browning machine guns, in the tail of the aircraft. This had the effect of partially eliminating one of the B-17's known and most glaring weaknesses. The vulnerability of the Flying Fortress's earlier variants to attack from the rear had been quickly discovered in combat, but both German and Japanese pilots seemed singularly slow in appreciating the difference between the Mark E and her elder sisters.

Other major, though less obvious changes, were worked into the aircraft. Except for the single nose gun (where retained) all machine guns were standardized with the 0.5in Browning. A twin set of machine guns were installed in a power-operated turret mounted just behind the flight deck and the radio compartment was adapted for the possible mounting of additional guns. The oddest feature of the new gunnery arrangements was the replacement of the ventral bath by a retractable power-operated turret just aft of the wings. This turret was operated by remote control, the gunner firing the guns from a periscopic position in the waist hatch. This novel arrangement proved impractical and was abandoned in favor of a Sperry ball turret, housing gunner and guns, after the 112th production model. This new arrangement was simultaneously worked into the B-17F. The gunner in this seemingly exposed position had to be small, but statistically his was one of the safest positions in the aircraft, despite its apparent vulnerability. One of his occupational hazards, however, was that in many bombers to be fitted with this turret, particularly the early ones, the door frame and the fittings of the turret proved inadequate.

Many other minor variations were worked into the aircraft by Boeing to counter various small problems, but it was the changes to the tail, fuselage and defensive armament that set the B-17E apart from the earlier B-17s. The radical changes resulted in a much stronger and better aircraft, a formidable bomber capable of further modification and improvement.

Above: **An action shot of a B-17E showing four of the Fortress's defensive positions – one ventral position, two dorsal positions and the waist gunner.**

Below: **The Boeing B-17E of 1941 was first flown on 5 September. Compared to earlier versions the Mark E was longer, had a larger fin area and carried better defensive armament. Armament improvements included dorsal and ventral power turrets and tail-gun position. A total of 512 were built by Boeing.**

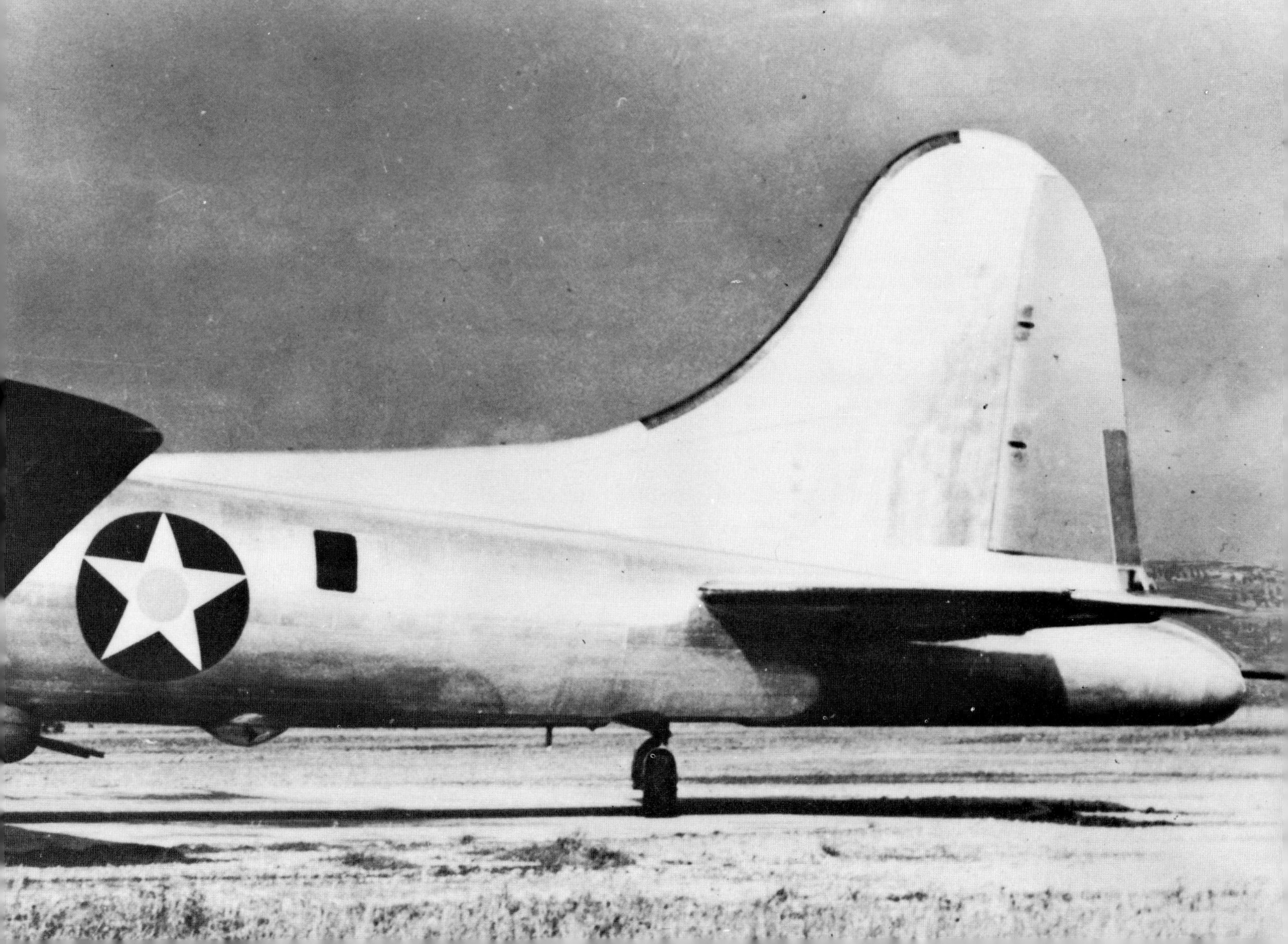

THE B-17F AND B-17G

While the B-17E had been a ton heavier than the B-17D and had shown no decline in performance this was not true of the B-17F. Another ton heavier, she was nearly 20mph slower than the Mark E, and roughly the same decline in speed was repeated in the B-17G over the B-17F. Yet despite their increased size and slower speeds both represented substantial qualitative advances over the B-17E and the decline of speed was not too great a handicap. With the operational speed of B-17s fixed at about 180mph any decline of the theoretically maximum speed of the aircraft was not particularly serious.

With the first of the B-17Fs coming off the production line just two days after the last of the B-17Es, some idea of the pace and urgency of American construction can be assessed by the fact that all the B-17F's tests had to be completed within one day before she was operationally assigned. In the spring of 1942, with the Germans and Japanese advancing on all fronts, there was no time for either prototypes or proper testing. Externally the first of the B-17Fs showed little change from the Mark E, but inwardly over 400 alterations were worked into the aircraft. These included self-sealing oil tanks, an improved oxygen system for the crew, more power sources, changes in the layout of the controls and better radio communications. Outwardly the most obvious change was the fitting of a single one-piece molded frameless Plexiglas nosepiece into which was slotted the flat bomb-aiming panel. New more powerful engines, the R-1820-97 with an emergency 1320hp rating, were installed along with carburetor intake dust filters and the wide paddle-bladed Hamilton Standard propellers. These were slightly longer but much broader than the propellers used up until that time. They were installed because they were more effective than the normal model under tropical conditions. The result of these combined modifications was to help push the weight of the loaded B-17F up to 65,500lb and this necessitated the strengthening of the undercarriage and the incorporating of a dual braking system.

One of the side effects of the Boeing-Douglas-Vega link-up was a natural tendency by the firms to work into their products their own idiosyncracies and modifications. It also allowed three sets of ideas to improve the aircraft to be in play at any one time. As a result many changes, peculiar to firms, were installed in B-17s. Mostly these were of a very minor nature, but they nevertheless demanded an involved system of numbering and lettering to show clearly what in-production modifications had been worked into specific aircraft. This, of course, was important in the correct allocation of spare parts for maintenance. Of the many modifications, however, one was of immense importance. In the 76th B-17F produced by Douglas a Bendix power-operated turret with twin 0.5in machine guns was mounted on the chin. This feature had been added as a result of combat experience with the second B-17F produced (No 41-24341). This aircraft had been specially fitted out as a heavy escort to the bombers and not as a bomber itself. Designated the XB-40, she was joined by fourteen Vega-built YB-40s. The standard armament of these aircraft differed from normal Fortresses by having an extra twin-gunned dorsal turret, double machine-gun posts in each of the waist positions and the Bendix chin turret. The idea behind these aircraft was for them to fly at the vulnerable extreme edges of bomber formations where their seemingly endless supply of ammunition could be used to best effect.

Above: **The B-17F in flight. Rushed into production and into service, the Mark F showed more than 400 alterations over the E version, most of which were internal. This version carried the Bendix chin turret.**

Unfortunately the weakness of the concept was that the escorts were too slow to cover the bombers effectively, particularly after the bombers had unloaded their bombs. In that state the bombers could easily outstrip their heavy escorts, burdened down as they were by abundant ammunition. Just as the tail turret had cut down one of the weaknesses of the B-17, the chin turret went some way to eliminate another. The majority of B-17Fs and all the B-17Gs incorporated the chin guns, but even these were not the full answer to the vulnerability of the Fortress to head-on attack. It was not so much defensive firepower that was weak in the B-17 – quite the reverse – but the aircraft's protection. Despite having some 27 pieces of armor and flak curtains worked into various parts of the aircraft, the lack of armor in the nose and the absence of bullet-proof glass were perennial weaknesses in the B-17. Perhaps the worst of the B-17s in this respect were the Mark Es. Many of the rear gunners were killed by fire not from aircraft they were engaging but from enemy fighters attacking from dead ahead. Their fire, raking the nose, often tore through the length of the fuselage before ripping out the rear turret and its crewman. Admittedly, better armor protection for both aircraft and individual members of the crew improved the situation, but the improvements were never really enough. The truth of the matter was that it was impossible to give the aircraft sufficient armor; it was impossible to produce an invulnerable aircraft.

With the B-17F the Americans had produced an aircraft extremely formidable in performance, defensive firepower, protection and bomb load, and a detailed examination of the ordnance and firepower of the B-17F is appropriate at this stage. Though the bomb-stowage arrangements of the B-17F differed from those used in earlier Marks, the normal bomb load remained 4000lb. But just as it had been possible for earlier B-17s to carry more than 4000lb, it was possible for the B-17F to carry a maximum load of 9600lb. Moreover, because the wings of the B-17F had been specially strengthened it was

Above and below left: Two photographs that show the most obvious external change worked into the F version of the Flying Fortress – the single-piece molded Plexiglas nose housing the bombardier's bombsight. This, of course, did nothing to cut down one of the major weaknesses of all B-17s, their vulnerability to head-on attack. Both Fortresses shown are early versions without a powered chin turret. *Below right:* The Cheyenne-type rear turret helped counterattack from another of the Fortress's most vulnerable quarters. Each gun had about 500 rounds per operation.

possible for her to lift a payload of 17,600lb and, in very exceptional circumstances, 20,800lb of ordnance. This weight of destruction could be lifted only because of the provision of special external racks that could be fitted to the aircraft by their ground crews. Though purpose-built the racks themselves were not factory fitted, but the bomb-release mechanism for the wing racks were naturally built into the aircraft during production. Some 2884 B-17Fs were thus fitted. The problem of massive payloads, except in a purpose-built machine, was that endurance fell away sharply. The heavier bomb loads were incompatible with the range requirements for aircraft attacking Germany from bases in Britain, but were useful in attacking tactical or even strategic targets in German-occupied western Europe. Under normal circumstances the bomb load of a Flying Fortress seldom exceeded 4000lb and in most operations would have been either 2600lb or less. Defensively the ammunition supplied to each aircraft and each gun varied, but it can be reasonably assessed at about 500 rounds per gun. Not altogether surprisingly, the best-supplied gunner was the rear gunner, but in stark terms, no gun on a B-17 carried more than one minute's supply of ammunition.

With the B-17F and its in-production modifications major improvements basically ceased. The B-17G was essentially the same as the later B-17Fs that carried the chin turrets and extra fuel tanks in the outer wing sections. The latter were the so-

Specifications for the B-17G

Wing Span	109ft 9in
Length	74ft 4in
Height	19ft 1in
Wing area	1,420sq ft

Weights:

Empty	36,135lb (16.13 tons)
Equipped	38,000lb (16.96 tons)
Normal Load	55,000lb (24.55 tons)
Maximum Normal Load	72,000lb (32.14 tons)

Power:
Four Wright Cyclone GR 1820-97 (R-1920-65) nine-cylinder air-cooled radial engines with Moss-General Electric turbo-superchargers. Each engine had 1,200hp at takeoff; emergency 1,320hp at 25,000ft. Engines ran at 2,300rpm. Four three-bladed Hamilton Standard propellers, 5ft 9½in in radius.

Fuel:

Normal	2,490 Imp Gallons
Maximum	3,569 Imp Gallons

Oil:
180 Imp Gallons

Range:

Maximum	4,400 statute miles on maximum fuel 3,300 statute miles on normal fuel

Ceiling:

Service	35,600ft

Speeds:

Maximum	300mph at 30,000ft
Maximum continuous speed	263mph at 25,000ft
Landing	74mph
Rate of Climb	37 minutes to 20,000ft

Bomb Load:
Depending on the types of bomb carried on a given mission the maximum normal load could be 2,600lb or 4,800lb or 6,000lb or 8,000lb. Maximum normal short-range bomb load was 17,600lb.

Armament:
Up to thirteen 0.5in machine guns, mostly concentrated in six positions.

Crew:
Ten

Above: **A Vega-built B-17G.**
Below: **Despite massive damage to the fuselage and outboard engine, the aircraft survived.**

called Tokyo tanks. There were some changes, but they were of a relatively minor nature. The nose compartment was slightly rearranged to allow the navigator marginally more room and the bomb-release mechanisms were slightly improved. The waist-gun windows were glazed over and the guns specially mounted. These last changes were very important for the crew members in the rear of the aircraft. With the later B-17Gs the fields of fire for the rear gunner were widened still further and the gunner was given a new reflector sight as a result of changes made at the Cheyenne Modification Center, Wyoming. These changes allowed the aircraft to be shortened by 5in. Thus, at the end of the war, an aircraft that had begun life as a solitary prototype, X-13372, way back in 1934–35, showed the following characteristics (see opposite).

Impressive though the technical data might be, the Flying Fortress in many ways belied her size. Inside she was a cramped, cold and awkward aircraft, completely unlike the B-29 which was de luxe in comparison. The B-17 demanded only the highest possible physical standards on the part of her crews. Sixty percent of the personnel screened by the RAF in 1941 for their twenty B-17Cs were rejected on medical grounds alone, being unable to withstand the effects of decompression and altitude sickness. Malfunctioning oxygen sets were always a danger, particularly in the earlier versions, with anoxia not uncommon. Frostbite was an occupational hazard for many of the crew, particularly the tail and waist gunners. Until excluded by the glazed windows of the B-17G, hurricane-force winds lashed the insides of the fuselage where temperatures could reach fifty below zero. The rear gunner, trapped on a small bicycle seat and padded knee holds, was particularly badly affected, but waist gunners faced the additional hazard of being thrown together and having their guns and ammunition belts entangled by violent gyrations of the aircraft. The radio room, the only part of the aircraft where a 6ft tall man could stand erect, could be as cold as the rear fuselage, and operators usually had to transmit wearing gloves. Only the five crew members in the nose had any real warmth, but of these only the pilots had any degree of comfort. The flight engineer's position was crouched and on a bicycle seat behind the pilots; that of the navigator, despite successive improvements, was cramped. The bombardier

Below left: **The B-17H, a modification of the B-17G, saw service in the Pacific and Atlantic. It was modified for air-sea rescue work, being fitted with a lifeboat that could be dropped on three parachutes to ditched crews. Note the Flying Boat behind the B-17H.**

Above: **B-17s were adapted for use in specific roles during the war. Here a B-17G with early warning radar for search purposes.**

shared with the pilots and gunners superb views, but he had to double as a gunner – and this he could not do in the critical run-in over the target.

Overall, none of the B-17s were comfortable aircraft, and movement within the aircraft was never easy. Movement along the rear fuselage, between the waist gunners, was by swaying rope-handled catwalks, and a similar situation prevailed in the bomb bays. Certain parts of the fuselage, particularly into the rear turret, could only be negotiated by the crawl. General movement between various parts of the aircraft seemed to be deliberately impeded rather than aided by the size and awkwardness of doors. But what the aircraft demanded in terms of physical discomfort, she paid back to her crew in rugged reliability. Though they were prone to flames the B-17s showed a remarkable ability to survive attacks that took out huge sections of wings, fuselage and tail. One Fortress survived an operation that resulted in over 2000 bullet holes being counted in its wings and fuselage. Many aircraft survived seemingly hopeless structural damage, while landing on feathered engines was almost a routine occurrence. There were many instances of novice pilots or even untrained crewmen improvising a flight home after the elimination of the two pilots, though this naturally was not that common. The B-17 was easy to fly and capable of absorbing massive damage: on these counts alone she secured and deserved her almost legendary reputation. Though the aircraft had its weaknesses, it is not altogether surprising that its overall robustness and airworthiness resulted in its seeing service in various specialist roles and in no less than eleven services.

Various B-17s, mostly of the later Marks, were converted for specific tasks and some of the older, tired survivors of many missions ended their days ferrying mail for the armies in the field. In the latter stages of the Pacific War many modern B-17s were pressed into service as troop carriers. Indeed, in the early stages of the Pacific War one of the first B-17Es, No 41-2593, was used as the personal transport aircraft of no less a person than General Douglas MacArthur. Many of the other conversions were for cargo transportation (one was for fuel) or for photographic reconnaissance. The 8th Air Force was assigned for a very brief period the 3rd PG, including one squadron of B-17s, but this group never saw service with the 8th and was sent to the Mediterranean. The Fortresses delegated to photographic reconnaissance in fact were considered too vulnerable to be used in combat zones, and most of their work was done in secondary theaters. Over fifty B-17Gs were converted to one vitally important role that was well out of the mainstream of B-17 activity. Designated the B-17H these aircraft were fitted out with a lifeboat that could be dropped on three parachutes to ditched aircrews. Such aircraft saw service both in the Pacific and in Europe.

Among the more bizarre activities to which certain B-17s were subjected was the BQ-7 project. Many war-weary B-17s were earmarked for experimental purposes, the object of which was to produce a radio-controlled flying bomb. The whole of the interior of the aircraft was gutted and then packed with 22,000lb of Torpex. The aircraft was manned by just two men, a pilot and a radio operator who primed the weapon. Both men had to bale out when their charge was activated. The idea was for the bomber to be guided in to its target by another bomber, but Project Castor, sometimes called Project Perilous, was abandoned after certain spectacular failures. One fully primed B-17 decided to embark upon an independent inspection of a major British industrial area before, oblivious to its controller, it wandered out to sea and self-destruction. Another B-17, out of control, made a crater 100ft wide in the countryside of East Anglia in a detonation that was heard thirty miles away. After these dangerous and unnecessary incidents the project was abandoned. The Allied superiority in conventional weapons was so great that there was no need to persist in work on unconventional weapons; that was something that could be left to the side lacking the strategic initiative.

It is ironic that after the early efforts of the US Navy to stifle the B-17 project, a B-17F should have been tested by the Navy during the war as a patrol bomber. In fact during the postwar years a number of B-17s saw service not only with the US Navy but with the Marine Corps and the Coast Guard. The B-17 also saw service in other foreign forces. The most important recipient, of course, was the RAF and various other Commonwealth air forces. After their unfortunate experiences with the Fortress I (B-17C) in 1941, the British received two more batches of B-17s (simply called Fortress II and Fortress III by the British) that together numbered 170 aircraft. Nearly all saw service either with Coastal Command or in an ECM role, but most finished serving as weather reconnaissance aircraft. Naturally for the purposes of strategic bombing the British preferred to use their own aircraft.

After the war Flying Fortresses saw service in various South American air forces, most notably those of Brazil and the Dominican Republic. In Europe they saw service with the French, Portuguese and Dutch air forces and in the War of 1948–49 for the establishment of the state of Israel some found

Above: **A B-17G-85-DC adapted as a test bed for a T-34 engine.**
Above right: **A B-17G in peacetime at Transpo-Dallas Airport.**
Right: **A ground radio-control unit of the 3225th Drone Squadron.**

their way into the Israeli Air Force. One Fortress actually bombed Cairo en route to Israel-Palestine, neither the crew nor the aircraft ever having been to the land for which they fought. Many, naturally, saw peaceful service. The Fortresses that were forced to land in Sweden were turned over to the Swedish government and SAS used them extensively as passenger airliners. Sweden was not alone in this. Various countries and minor American companies used Fortresses either on feeder or main routes. Mostly, however, the survivors that were kept on after the war were used either as freight carriers or for surveys. A handful are still believed to be in service, but the fate of most Fortresses soon after the end of the European war was simple and straightforward. They were scrapped, in their thousands. Hands of men less able than those that built, maintained and fought them achieved what enemy action had signally failed to achieve in war.

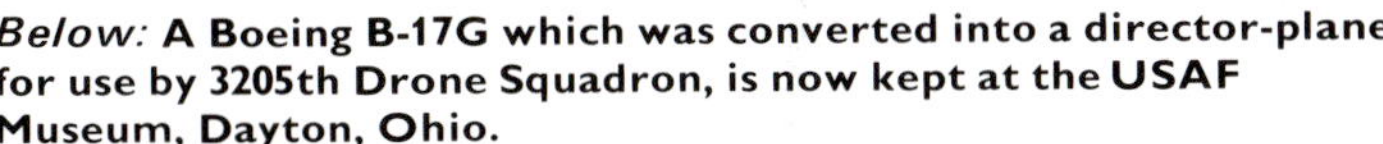

Below: **A Boeing B-17G which was converted into a director-plane for use by 3205th Drone Squadron, is now kept at the USAF Museum, Dayton, Ohio.**

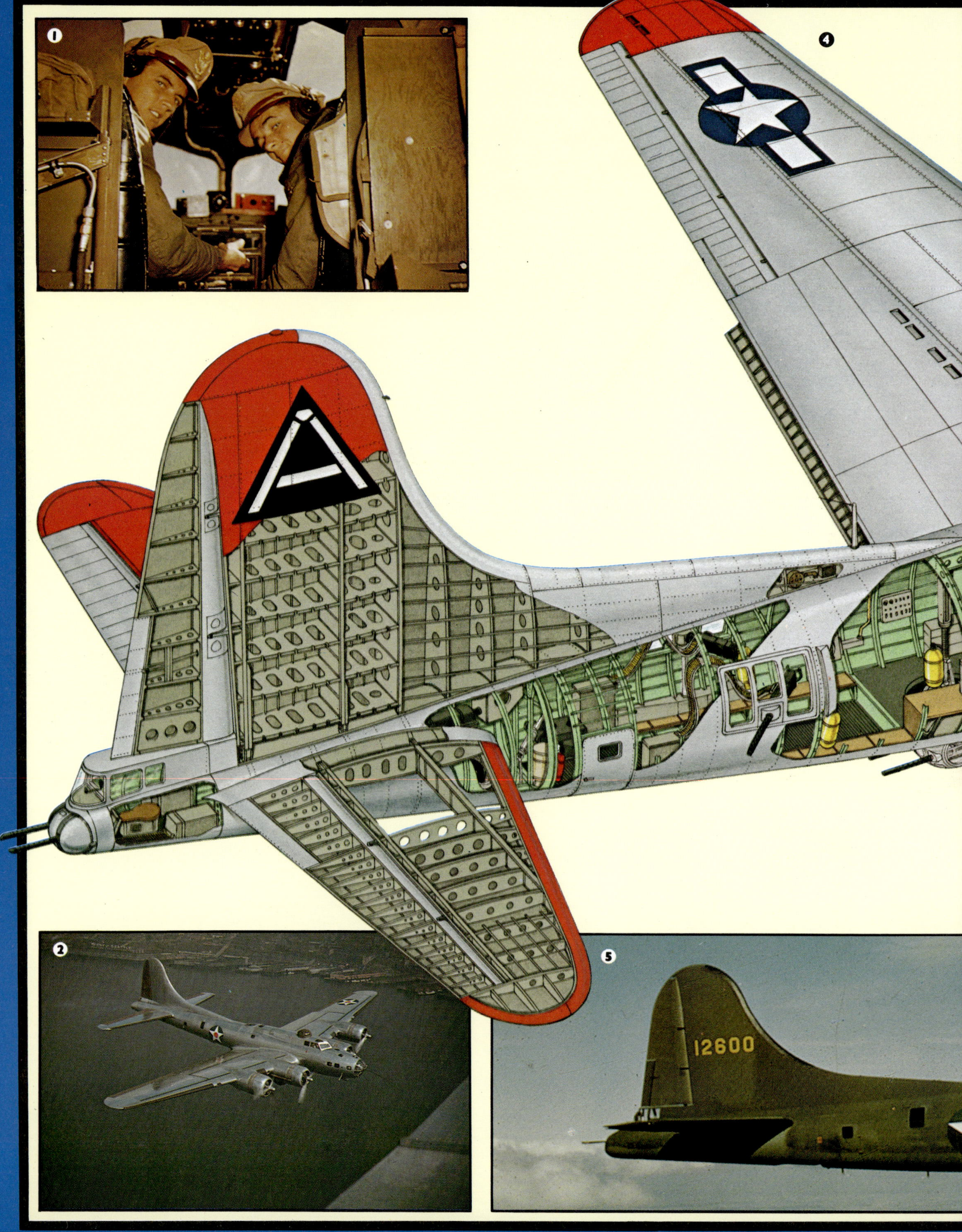
1
4
2
5
12600

1. The cramped cockpit of a B-17.
2. A B-17E during 1941.
3. A waist gunner on the ready over North Africa, 1943.
4. A Boeing B-17G of the 401st Bombardment Squadron, 91st Bombardment Group, 1st Combat Bombardment Wing, of the US 8th AF.
5. A B-17E.

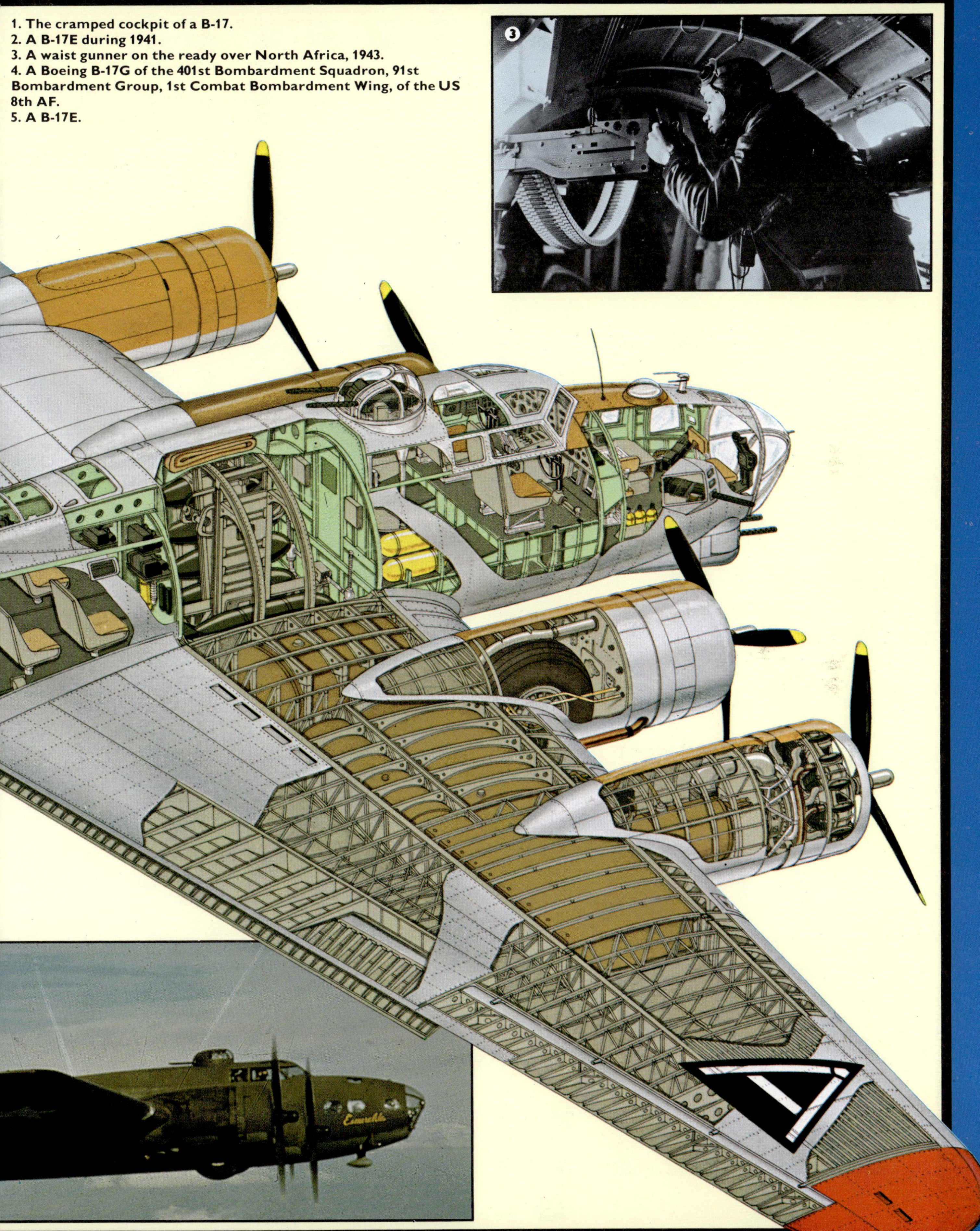

1. Captain Charles Hudson in the nose of his plane.
2. Sergeant Barraza, gunner and radio operator in position at the waist gun.
3. Crew positions in a B-17F.
4. A B-17F of the 324th Bombardment Squadron, 91st Bombardment Group, of the US 8th AF.

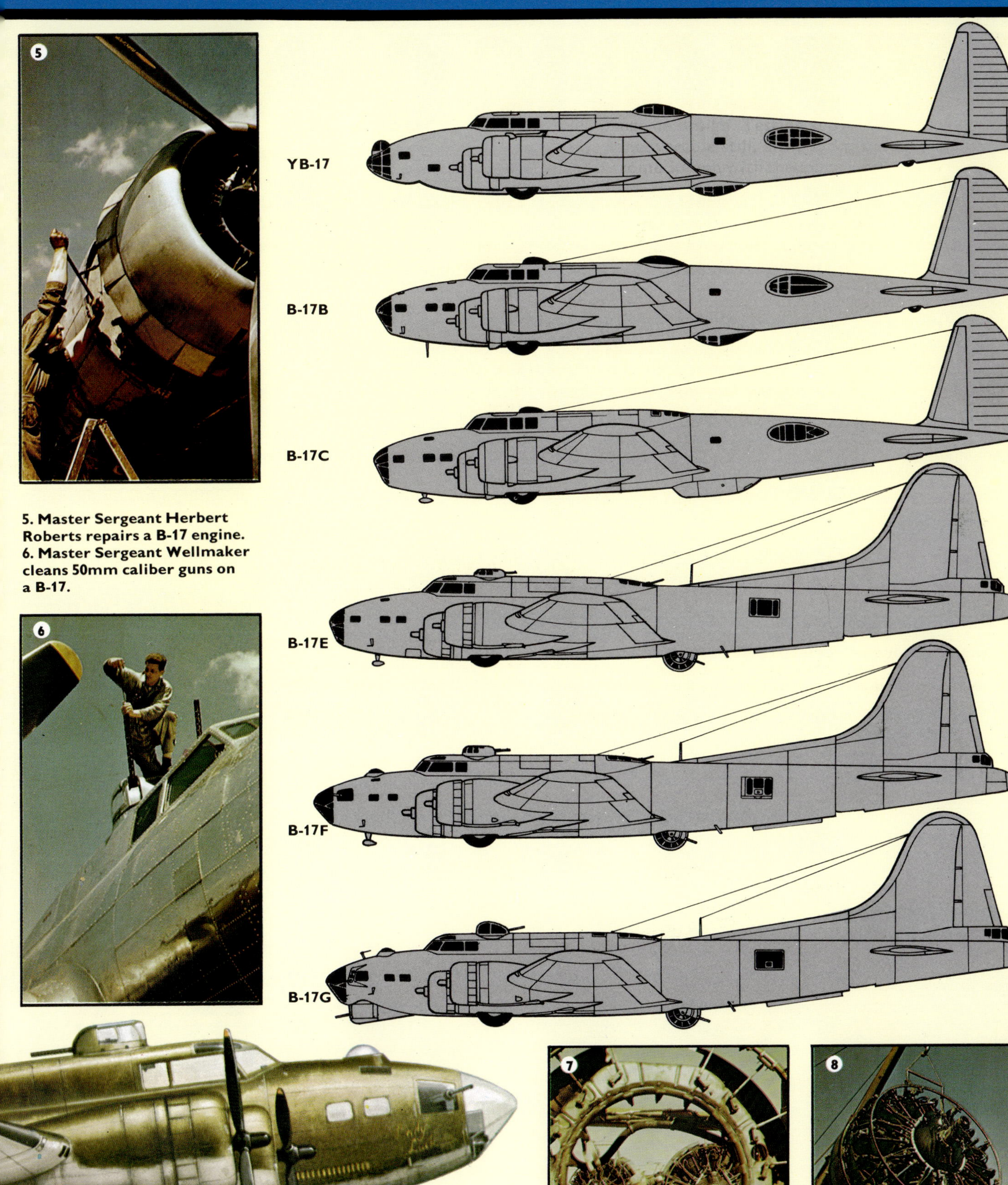

5. Master Sergeant Herbert Roberts repairs a B-17 engine.
6. Master Sergeant Wellmaker cleans 50mm caliber guns on a B-17.

7. Master Sergeant Harrell Farrah seen through the engine cowling of a B-17.
8. A new engine is hoisted into position.

THE PACIFIC CAMPAIG

The coming of war to the USA in December 1941 found the USAAF in the Pacific in no position to counter the well-planned Japanese attack throughout Southeast Asia. Given the weakness of the US Asiatic Fleet (a paper or prestige force rather than a properly balanced fighting force) and the inferiority of the US Pacific Fleet to the Combined Fleet of the Imperial Japanese Navy, the Americans, in the absence of large ground forces, had to rely on air power as their only means of countering Japanese movements once the policy of deterrence had failed to prevent the Japanese from going to war. The problem for the Americans, however, was that even in the air their forces were totally inadequate to meet the Japanese challenge. In December 1941 the USAAF had only 150 B-17s of which only fifty were the combat-worthy B-17Es. Only one-third of all the Fortresses were in the vast expanses of the Pacific. The USAAF had but a motley collection of 131 aircraft on Hawaii. Of this total there were only twelve B-17Cs and Ds, part of the 5th BG. In the Philippines the Army deployed 176 aircraft and two Bombardment Groups, the 7th and the 19th. But the 7th was effectively in cadre form, awaiting reinforcement from the USA, while the 19th was drastically understrength. Between them the two groups mustered just 35 Flying Fortresses, none of them B-17Es.

The opening of the war immediately reduced the already low strength of the Fortresses. Five were lost during the opening attack on Pearl Harbor and fourteen were destroyed on the ground when the Japanese launched their first strikes on the Philippines. The brunt of the effort to hold the Japanese fell on the depleted forces in the Philippines because the aircraft on Hawaii were too far away either to be of assistance or to carry the fight to the Japanese elsewhere. Though on 10 December 1941 the B-17s in the Philippines carried out the first American bombing raid of the war – an unsuccessful series of attacks on the Japanese invasion fleet bound for Luzon – a steady attrition forced the Americans to pull all their surviving aircraft out from the Philippines by the end of the month.

The surviving B-17s were withdrawn to Australia where only ten were found fit to resume combat duties. These were rapidly redeployed to Java, since they were the only Allied aircraft capable of offering serious resistance to the Japanese invasion of the Netherlands East Indies. Until the capitulation of the Indies in March 1942 these aircraft, plus reinforcements rapidly sent out from the USA, tried in vain to stem the Japanese advance. By the end of the campaign some eighty B-17s had been concentrated and fought in the theater, 49 in Java

Below: **The nine-man crew of a B-17D pose beside their aircraft after a mission at their base at Maceeba, Queensland, Australia. They formed part of the 64th Bombardment Squadron, 43rd Bombardment Group.**

itself. The results achieved by these aircraft were singularly unimpressive. Of the 49 on Java thirty were lost. Nineteen had been destroyed on the ground, but only six had been lost in combat with Japanese aircraft. Of the eighty in the theater, 52 were lost and a further six had to be written off as a result of accidents in Australia. Postwar analysis was to show that in the 350 missions flown by the B-17s in the opening phase of the war only two Japanese ships were sunk, a meager return for much bravery. Not unnaturally the paucity of success was not appreciated at the time, reports of successes being greatly exaggerated and far in excess of actual achievements.

In large part the poor showing of the B-17 in this phase of the war stemmed from factors beyond its control. The Flying Fortress was really in an impossible situation. It was an offensive, strategic weapon, but in 1942 it had to try to be a defensive, tactical weapon. Understrength at the start of the war and suffering unacceptably high losses in the opening phase of hostilities, the reinforcements sent out from the USA – in the form of the 43rd BG – could be used only to bolster the depleted 7th and 19th. Reinforcements were too few in number and too widely spread in area and time to permit their being in a position to exercise some direct influence in the battle area. Some 53 aircraft were dispatched from the eastern seaboard of the USA where the 43rd was based. These aircraft were forced to fly via the Caribbean, Africa and India to reach their operational areas, and perhaps it is remarkable that of the total only nine never made it. Many of the aircraft sent had come directly from the factories and desperately needed servicing and maintenance, which were not available, when they arrived in Java and Australia. The crews, too, were raw, and it was many months after its arrival in the theater that it can be said that the 43rd was properly constituted. By that time, however, the 7th had been redeployed to India in an effort to try to hold the Japanese advance in Burma while the 19th, taking crews and aircraft from the 7th, reconcentrated in Australia. By the time the rearrangement of the B-17s had been completed, however, the flood tide of Japanese conquest had been largely brought to a halt, though it continued to edge its way forward in certain areas for some time afterward. In May 1942 at Coral Sea American carrier forces had checked the Japanese advance in the Southwest Pacific, forcing the enemy to recast plans for the reduction of Port Moresby and eastern New Guinea. In June the cream of Japanese naval aviation, the carrier forces, was annihilated at the Battle of Midway. Only in the latter battle did B-17s participate, but their intervention was negligible. In both battles it was Ameri-

Below: **The bombing of Hickham Field, Oahu, Hawaiian Islands on the morning of Sunday 7 December 1941. At the time of the Japanese attack on Pearl Harbor only 12 Fortresses were on Oahu, and three are shown.**

can carrier-based aircraft, particularly the dive bombers, that wreaked havoc, not the land-based aircraft.

After Coral Sea and Midway the Japanese attempted to consolidate their initial gains by a series of movements through the Bismarck Archipelago, into the Solomons, their aim being to outflank Australia and to achieve its isolation from supplies and reinforcements drawn from the USA. After these two successes, however, the Americans were in a position to counter such moves with their sea and land forces, landing in August 1942 on the Japanese-held island of Guadalcanal. In this effort the B-17s played a significant role, because by September the USAAF deployed four Groups in the area. To shore up the defenses there the 5th and 11th Groups from Hawaii were deployed to the New Hebrides, the 35-strong 11th arriving in New Caledonia in July. These forces formed part of the hastily-constituted 13th Air Force. Those forces in Australia were part of the 5th Air Force. Between them the four groups in September 1942 reached their peak strength of about 155 aircraft. The process of reinforcement had indeed been massive, far higher than these simple figures would suggest. Losses, from all causes, had to be covered, and such was the strain on shipping resources at this critical juncture of the war and such was the crucial importance of time, that many B-17s had to be employed as load-carriers in order to keep their sisters in service. It was paradoxical that the reinforcement of the theater with B-17s came at a time when it had already been decided to phase out the aircraft from the Pacific theater. In the vast area of the Pacific the Liberator, with its slightly longer range, was preferred to the Fortress, and after October 1942 the process of breaking up units and the re-equipment of new and existing formations with the B-24 began. By the beginning of 1943 the Fortresses no longer carried the weight of the American counteroffensive in the air, but it was not until September 1943 that the 5th and 11th Groups flew their last Fortress mission. Even in the Aleutians the limited numbers of Fortresses were gradually reduced to nothing. By November 1943, apart from command transports, only one B-17 remained in service in the whole of the Pacific area. Nevertheless, for all the time the B-17s were on station they carried the fight to the Japanese, mainly in the form of attacks on harbors and shipping. Success, as we have seen, was scant, though the 43rd was heavily involved in the devastatingly successful Battle of the Bismarck Sea (March 1943) which resulted in the annihilation of a Japanese military convoy bound for the upper Solomons. This battle in effect doomed Japanese efforts to hold the area.

For the most part, however, the record of the B-17 was not convincing, though it must be stated that after the introduction of the B-17E, complete with tail gunners, Japanese aircraft showed a healthy respect for the aircraft. In fact the new generation B-17s showed that the new Flying Fortresses could look after themselves in fights with Japanese interceptors. The small-caliber guns used by Japanese fighters made it very difficult for them to shoot down the heavy bomber, while their own lack of armor and self-sealing fuel tanks made them very vulnerable to 0.5in gunfire. Had the B-17s remained in the Pacific then, their success may well have been as great as that of those aircraft that replaced them. But the sad fact of the matter for the B-17 was that throughout its period of service in the Pacific it labored under far too many handicaps to be really effective. Probably the most critical weakness lay in the fact that on all too many occasions the B-17s were forced to go into action in very small numbers. For most of this period of the Pacific War for a squadron to be at fifty percent strength – in effect five or more aircraft – was little short of miraculous. For a whole group to attack with five aircraft was normal; for a group to attack with anything more than that number really was an exceptional feat. Against land targets such numbers were totally inadequate while to attack shipping in such strength was almost derisory. Even when attacking in formation – an inverted Vee – in order to pattern the bombs in a straddle, the chances of hitting a ship were very small. On far too many occasions the B-17s were called upon to commit themselves to actions at the extreme edge of their endurance, thus lessening the amount of bombs that could be carried and, as a result, lessening the chances of a successful operation. Indeed, in many such attacks it can be quite reasonably argued that had the Japanese been better equipped, particularly with early-warning radar, far heavier losses would have been inflicted on the attacking B-17s than in fact were the case. Even allowing for the defensive firepower of the Fortress and the vulnerability and poor performance of the Zero-sen at high altitudes, the smallness of American attacks always ran the risk of defeat in detail, and perhaps the Americans were fortunate to escape without heavier losses.

Allowance has to be made for other factors when assessing the performance of the B-17 in the Pacific. It was the aircraft's misfortune to be involved in a catastrophic defeat. The B-17 was the major weapon in the aerial armory at a time of chaos and disorganization. It lived a hand-to-mouth existence on rough-hewn jungle strips, without proper maintenance, often having to stage through equally or even more primitive airstrips in order to reach objectives. It had to contend with appalling climatic conditions. The alternating heat and rain, bringing dust and mud in turn, made servicing a nightmare. In the air the bombers could encounter cloud and storms of ferocious violence that stretched the width of the horizon and over which they could not climb. It is not without significance that in seven months of operations the 11th BG lost six Fortresses to enemy action and twelve to the weather. One raid by three B-17s actually resulted in 100 percent losses when the aircraft could not find their way through a weather front and had to ditch in the sea as the fuel tanks spluttered dry. Overall the Pacific experience was an unfortunate one for the B-17, though the odds were heavily stacked against it from the start. As a result it left the area not properly or fairly tested because at no time in its operations had it been able to act en masse strategically. That test, for the B-17, was to be in Europe.

Right: **Following a bombing raid on New Guinea, the crew of a Flying Fortress clean the plane's guns.**
Below: **A B-17C which was preserved after the war.**

All pictures: **Shots of a B-17G85DL which has been preserved. Some 42 B-17s have survived to the present day and are kept by museums and enthusiasts.**

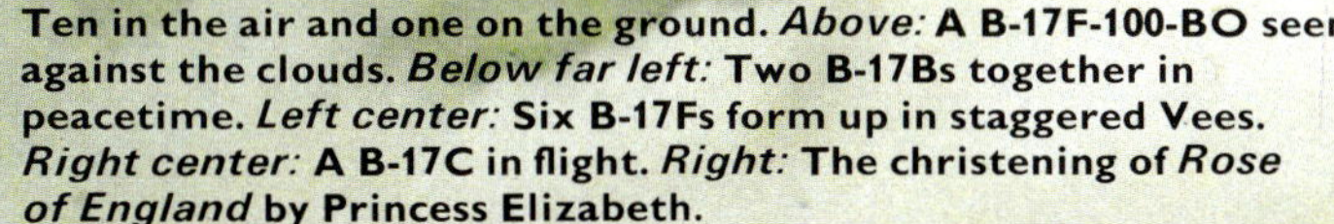

Ten in the air and one on the ground. *Above:* A B-17F-100-BO seen against the clouds. *Below far left:* Two B-17Bs together in peacetime. *Left center:* Six B-17Fs form up in staggered Vees. *Right center:* A B-17C in flight. *Right:* The christening of *Rose of England* by Princess Elizabeth.

THE EUROPEAN CAM

Even before the American entry into the war in December 1941, Anglo-American strategic discussions had resulted in the decision that the primary Allied effort would be directed against Germany, the most powerful and dangerous of the three Axis powers. In order to defeat Germany the USA promised full land, sea and air participation in the joint Anglo-American effort, but the USAAF had arrogated for itself the role of bombing Germany into surrender. Both the USAAF and RAF Bomber Command claimed that given sufficient aircraft they could conduct a strategic bombing offensive that would bring Germany to her knees though they had very different ideas of how to bring this about. Nevertheless, before the war and before the differences of tactical doctrine became apparent, it was assumed that even while the USA mobilized her full resources for war prior to embarking upon major land and sea operations against the Germans, the USAAF would be able to build up forces quickly in Britain and soon assume a major part in a joint bombing campaign.

Matters did not work out as easily as that. To simplify a rather complicated story one can argue that 1942 was a year largely concerned with training, deployment and initial, limited operations; 1943 was the year of repeated attempts to make the theory of strategic bombing work without adequate resources. In 1944 the main effort of the USAAF to make its policies work was frustrated by the need to divert air resources toward support for the forthcoming invasion of France. It was only in the latter part of 1944 and in 1945 that the Americans had the forces needed to conduct a full-scale strategic bombing campaign, and by that time it was really too late to prove that the concept was workable. Air enthusiasts who had claimed that strategic bombing could end a war by itself and do away with the need for such mundane matters as invasions and land battles always had to contend with the unpalatable fact that the American air offensive against Germany had to be halted several times, most notably in October 1943, after the bombers had taken unacceptably high losses. In 1943 in fact the Germans were destroying the British and American strategic bombers far more rapidly than they could be replaced, and far more quickly than they could inflict commensurate and significant damage on Germany. To put the matter simply: in 1943 the Luftwaffe beat the bombers; strategic bombing failed. Subsequently, the air enthusiasts had to contend with the equally awkward fact that two out of every three bombs dropped on Germany in the course of the war fell after the Normandy invasion – for which, if their arguments had been correct, there would have been no need.

There was, however, a reverse side to this rather bleak coin. What remained hidden from the Allies during the years of war was the fact that their campaigns had a cumulative effect, and what they had said bombing would achieve was in fact achieved, but over a much longer time scale than had been anticipated. The true effectiveness of bombing was obscured in the end by the rapidity and totality of Germany's defeat. Hitler's armies fought their last battles almost without fuel as a result of Allied air attacks; they fought over a country whose economy lay in ruins as a result of many factors, but the most obvious and important was the carnage wrought from the skies. It must be noted that strategic bombing achieved the neutralization and isolation of the industrialized Ruhr. In normal circumstances this would have been rightly hailed as a remarkable achievement, but the fact that within one week of its isolation the Ruhr was surrounded and mopped up by land forces took the edge off the air forces' success. It more or less went unnoticed in a series of successes that by that time had reached avalanche proportions. Success really came too late to justify fully the concept of strategic bombing.

The activities of the B-17 and the concept of strategic bombing were intimately related and to understand them both, and

Below: **Two B-17G 75-BO Fortresses and a combination of Douglas- and Boeing-built B-17Gs practice box-formation flying over southern England.**
Right: **The bombing of Schweinfurt, the raid of 14 October 1943.**

AIGN

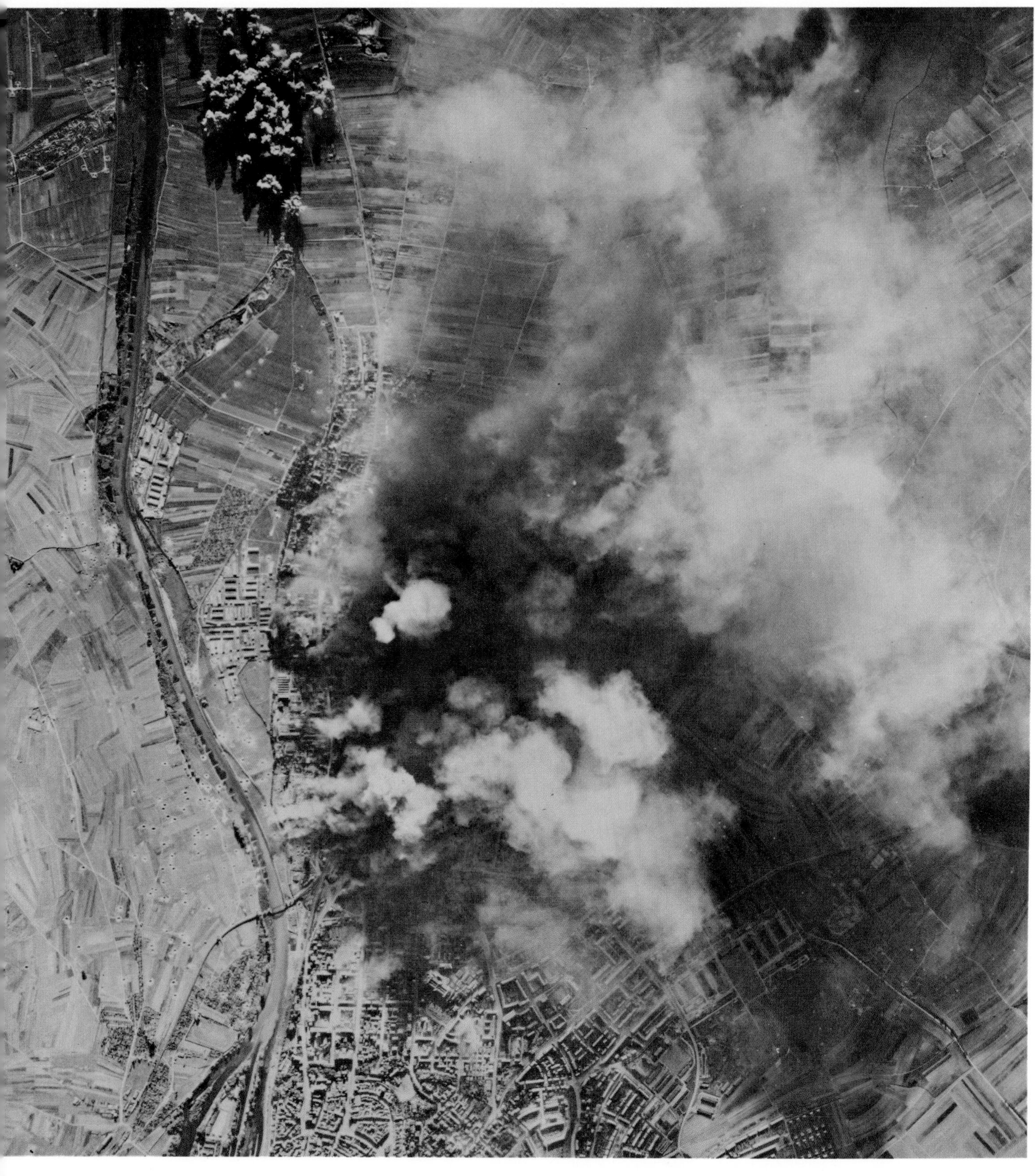

to comprehend the part that the B-17 played in strategic bombing, one must first really redefine what the USAAF sought to achieve and then why success proved elusive until too late in the war for the concept to be really successful. The essence of the American case for strategic bombing rested on the belief that, used en masse for mutual protection, heavy bombers such as the Flying Fortress could launch a series of devastatingly accurate attacks on key industrial centers, thus paralyzing enemy production and bringing about the collapse of his war effort. To achieve the required accuracy and scale of destruction the Americans had to use their aircraft in concentrated formations in daylight. Given the primitiveness of air navigation, night bombing could not hope to strike the key centers singled out by the Americans for destruction. The British had tried night precision bombing between 1940 and 1941; they realized its inherent inaccuracies and abandoned such tactics in favor of general attacks on built-up areas in February 1942.

The Americans, however, had certain very good reasons for wanting to go their own way. The American airmen were astute enough to realize that in any war economy there were certain very vulnerable bottlenecks which could be crippled by heavy air attacks. Among such bottlenecks they identified the submarine construction yards, the aircraft industry, the ball-bearing industry, oil, the synthetic rubber and military vehicles industries. Subsequently the Americans were to appreciate the value of sustained attacks on the transportation network. The Americans knew that if their attacks were to be successful then targets such as these had to be attacked during the day. In addition, the USAAF was adamant in its advocacy

Above: **B-17s of the 8th AF line up on their runways for a mission.**
Top right: **Fortresses of the 15th AF hit Ploesti oil targets, 24 April 1944.**
Bottom right: **Major General Ira C Eaker and Lieutenant General Carl Spaatz, in London, 1 January 1944.**

of this concept for 'political' reasons. A successful strategic bombing policy alone could justify the independent role the Army Air Force sought. The USAAF desired a genuinely recognized separate identity from the US Army and the US Navy. It also wanted to be clearly separated from RAF Bomber Command; it rightly feared being subordinated to the British effort. This was where the B-17 entered the picture. It was primarily the Flying Fortress, but with the Liberator as the second string, that was the means of putting into effect the policy of strategic bombing. The B-17 was the main means by which the USAAF intended to bring about the defeat of its four enemies – the Germans, the British and the US Army and Navy; and Flying Fortress was the aircraft in which the AAF placed its trust.

The reasons why the Americans failed to achieve the strategic victory over Germany in the manner they anticipated were many and complex, and in this book only certain of those reasons, most relevant to the story of the B-17, will be discussed. A major factor was the extraordinary degree of elasticity in an economy. The German transportation system is a microscopic example of the problem that the Americans faced. The Americans had many hesitations about the wisdom of bombing the transportation system. They feared that transportation would prove too resilient, too flexible. They suspected that ways around damage could always be improvised.

In part this hesitation was correct, but only in part. Experience was to show that even so flexible a transport system as that of Germany could be brought to utter ruination, but in general the American fear was well founded. The transportation system can be applied across the board to the whole of German industry. The dispersal of industry across a vast territory, the 'hardening' of specially sensitive centers and the efficiency of German repair and maintenance systems meant that the extent of damage inflicted by bombing was minimized and absorbed far more readily than had been anticipated.

A second factor directly related to this was the lack of co-operation the USAAF received from RAF Bomber Command. Air Chief Marshal Arthur Harris, whose true abilities and worth have never received proper recognition, was correctly skeptical of many American claims, but this hardly justified his pointed refusals to tie in British raids far more closely with the American effort than in fact was the case. Nominally the Allies were to co-ordinate their efforts in order to bomb Germany 'around the clock.' In raids that were supposed to complement one another and to throw the greatest possible strain on German resources, the British were supposed to bomb by night targets that blended with those sought out by the Americans during the day. As early as 25 September 1943 the Deputy Chief of the Air Staff (British) commented critically on the refusal of Harris to bomb certain targets as he had been ordered. These cities were centers of the German aircraft industry, against which American efforts were then directed. For the most part, however, Harris went his own way. This was a major handicap to the American effort, though in fairness it must be said that American complaints against Harris were few. In any case, had the American concepts been valid in the first place, there would have been no need for any form of support from the RAF for American operations.

Another major handicap was the weather. The Americans had been trained for bombing from high altitudes, for which they were equipped with a very good sight. But the vagaries of the European weather frequently resulted in missions being cancelled or aborted or bombs being dropped more or less at random. To be effective strategic bombing had to be continuous because its toll was, by its very nature, attritional. There were many reasons – losses, maintenance difficulties, crew fatigue, the need to change targets in order to retain surprise but still afford relief to those places already attacked – that made it very difficult to maintain the high tempo of operations needed to ensure success. Of all these material factors possibly the most important one remained the weather, which often afforded German industry protection that the Luftwaffe could not provide.

By far the most important factors in the shortcomings of the American concept of strategic bombing lay in the flaws inherent in the theory itself and the weapons with which the theory was supposed to be put into practice. The American idea envisaged a heavy bomber fighting its way to and from the objective. The harsh reality of the situation was that no bomber, however well armed or protected, could hope to operate successfully deep inside air space controlled by enemy fighters. Conditions of air superiority had to be assured if the bombers were to be effective. The bombers themselves could not hope to fight for and secure air supremacy, yet this was in effect what was being asked of them. The Fortress, in formation, was capable of about 180mph on its outward journey, and was far more vulnerable than the Americans had either imagined or feared. The Americans had reasoned that by flying at heights of five or six miles the worst of the flak could be avoided. This was more or less correct, but did have the drawback that the target was often covered by clouds. The Americans also reasoned that by flying in tight formation the massive array of 0.5in machine guns could beat off enemy fighters. This was to prove manifestly false. Losses were inflicted on German fighters, but never to the extent claimed and never on the scale necessary to wrest air superiority from the Germans. The Fortress, as any bomber, had to be provided with escorts, fighters that were prepared to fight for and secure air superiority over the enemy homeland if bombing was to prove effective. This was the fatal mistake that the USAAF made in the early years of the war; it assumed that the Fortress could command the skies through which it flew.

Moreover, certain matters directly relating to the Fortress and its performance must be made clear if one is to make any serious assessment of the B-17 and its wartime activities. It may seem incredible in the light of the fact that American industry produced over 98,000 aircraft for the USAAF – of which over 12,000 were Fortresses, over 15,000 were Mustangs and over 19,000 were Liberators – but for most of the war the American air forces operating in Europe were acutely short of aircraft. It was only in the spring and summer of 1944 that the strategic forces, the 8th and 15th Air Forces, grew into their strength, and even after that time much of their activities had to be directed toward tactical objectives. For most of the war American strategic bomber strength was very marginal to requirements. It was only in 1944, after massive reinforcement and a drastic reduction of losses as a result of the Mustang's successful fight for air superiority over Germany, that the Americans possessed the strength to mount a prolonged bombing campaign.

The lack of numerical strength was compounded by the relative lightness of the payload of the Flying Fortress. It was a sad fact of life that as good as the Fortress was as an aircraft and as a bomber, she lacked a commensurate punch for her size and crew requirements that mass attacks could not always make good. However, one must balance the scales somewhat with the observation that without her the Americans could not have mounted a strategic air offensive in the first place. The Fortress played a vital role, but in the end not quite in the manner intended.

The initial wartime agreement between the British and Americans (14 January 1942) envisaged the rapid build-up of the USAAF in Britain. On 27 January Major General Carl Spaatz was appointed to command the 8th Air Force, the unit earmarked to carry out the strategic bombing of Germany from Britain. Less than a month later, on 20 February, the commander of the 8th Air Force's Bomber Command, Brigadier General Ira C Eaker, arrived in Britain. The American objective was to concentrate in Britain a force of sixty combat groups, totalling 3500 aircraft, by the spring of 1943. Of this total 33 were to be Bombardment Groups, of which seventeen were to be heavy, ten medium and six light. By definition at this time the majority of the heavy Groups were to consist of Flying Fortresses.

A series of events was to conspire to frustrate American intentions. The Pacific situation deteriorated with such rapidity in 1942 that, despite the 'Germany first' policy, resources had to be sent first to the Pacific in order to stabilize the situation there. It was only after the Japanese had been checked that the USAAF could really begin to concentrate upon Europe, but North Africa siphoned off much strength that should have gone to Britain. The critical, though passing, danger to the British position in the Middle East in 1942 resulted in the deployment of initial USAAF strength to Egypt – from where the Americans launched their first daylight precision raid of the war against the Ploesti oil fields in Rumania. This commitment was extended by the demands of the

Torch landings in North Africa in October 1942. The AAF had to commit substantial forces to give tactical support to the land armies during this crucial phase of operations. The Mediterranean ulcer was to sap any concentration on British soil throughout the whole of 1943 because the bombers, once in the Mediterranean Theater of Operations, were naturally retained there to meet the Army's demands for support in the invasions of Sicily, Salerno and Anzio. In large measure the success of these invasions can be traced to the paralysis of German communications by the bombers. Although used tactically for much of the time, the strategic bombing campaign was to benefit in the long term by the involvement of the bombers in the MTO. Once the Italian campaign settled down to a long slogging match across the various mountain valleys, the US 15th Air Force was ideally placed to wage a bombing offensive against southern Germany (inclusive of Austria) and the Balkans. Not only was shuttle bombing carried out between the MTO and Britain, but also between Italy and southern Russia, and the latter was not really very successful. The Soviet authorities seemed indifferent to the needs and demands inherent in co-operation if such operations were to be of value, and in one brilliant opportunist attack the Luftwaffe caught and destroyed 41 Flying Fortresses on the ground, damaging still more. Nevertheless, these were minor affairs, and despite many reverses and difficulties the 15th Air Force played an increasingly significant role in the strategic bombing of Germany from 1944 onward.

The Americans' main effort was to be made where they encountered the greatest difficulties – with the 8th Air Force in Britain. The most serious of all its problems involved the physical movement of personnel and equipment to Britain and the construction of adequate facilities in UK. Airfields had to be built on a massive scale and each airfield was a major undertaking in its own right. There was no question of using grass runways for heavily loaded bombers. Airfields, therefore, had to have three concrete runways and perimeter track with dispersal points. Concrete requirements for a single airfield represented a sixty-mile road, eighteen feet wide. The first American-built airfield took ten months to complete, required 1,500,000 man-days and cost $5 million. Given just this single consideration it is not surprising that by the end of 1942 only nine of the heavy Groups assigned to the 8th should have entered service; that one group was one complete squadron understrength and that another Group, the 93rd, should have been temporarily in North Africa. Two other groups, the 97th and 301st, were also detached from the 8th Air Force by the end of 1942. Thus only six groups were in the UK after one year of war, and with a group theoretically carrying four squadrons each of twelve aircraft, the extent of American weakness can be appreciated. To train air and ground crews, to move them to their ports of embarkation, to transport the ground elements across the Atlantic in the fast monster liners and then to settle into hastily-built bases in an alien land was a mammoth task. The sheer logistics of such a move were immense, and it must be recalled that this was just the start. The Americans had to sustain themselves; every item of military equipment had to be shipped across the Atlantic at the height of the German submarine offensive. All nonmilitary essentials similarly had to be ferried across the ocean because British resources were inadequate to fill American needs. To gauge the depth of the American difficulty it is worth noting that for them to mount a 500-bomber raid a pool of at least 1250 aircraft had to be available to allow for maintenance and repair of battle damage. To put 500 bombers into the air demanded a back-up of 75,000 officers and men, 300 tons of operational equipment, plus fuel and bombs, and a standing reserve of 8500 tons of spare parts. Given the enormity of the overheads involved, the relative slowness of the American build-up of strategic bombers in Britain can be understood. The development of the strength of the heavy bomber element within the 8th Air Force can best be represented by the chart in the Appendix.

Below: **Return to the scene of a defeat. Flying Fortresses of the 8th AF attacking ball-bearing plants, railroad yards, warehouses and machine shops at Schweinfurt on 13 April 1944.**

OPERATIONS AND TAC

With the first B-17 flying into Polebrook on 6 July 1942, the 8th Air Force was able to launch its first all-American bombing operation on 17 August when twelve B-17Fs of 97th BG, under the command of Colonel Frank A Armstrong, Jr, raided the marshalling yards at Rouen. Eaker also flew on the raid which was aided by a diversionary sortie of six Fortresses designed to draw German defenses away from Rouen. The deception was successful and all Armstrong's aircraft returned safely, having inflicted damage on the objective.

For the remainder of the year the 8th Air Force continued to mount operations ever deeper into German-occupied territory. It was not until 27 January 1943, when again under Armstrong (by then commander of the 306th), that American bombers first flew against the Reich itself. The first German city to be attacked by Fortresses was the port of Wilhelmshaven, and the Americans lost three bombers. Up until that time American losses had been small with 32 aircraft (or two percent) being lost between Rouen and the end of the year. However, there were two catches in this situation. Firstly, the Americans were working on a shoestring in terms of aircraft and air crews. With North Africa taking aircraft away from Britain, the losses were sufficiently heavy – the size of an understrength 1942 group – to cause operations to be suspended in late 1942 on two separate occasions. Secondly, the initial raids were really only the most shallow of penetrations of enemy airspace, and the Americans were not slow to read the danger signs. Though numerical losses had been light, no single raid had carried either weight or depth. German reaction time, despite the radar warnings of aircraft forming up over southern England, was short, and the bombers usually had escort cover as they crossed the dangerous coast. The Americans, who were naturally shaken by their first losses, recognized the perils they faced if they were to conduct strategic operations that involved deep penetrations of German airspace. Such operations necessarily involved many hours of flight over the main centers of enemy strength without the benefit of fighter cover. The optimists remained unshaken, but the first contact with the enemy convinced everyone that the tactical doctrine of the bombers had to be recast in order to improve the survival chances of the bombers and to enhance their prospects of inflicting serious damage on objectives.

Throughout the war the Americans were forced to alter

Right: **Bombing through cloud: the contrails, visible 50 miles away, were frozen icicles that formed some 30ft astern of the exhausts.**
Below right: **A B-17 is lost with its crew over Berlin.**
Below: **The Box Formation with B-17s in Vees and stacked to give mutual support.**

ICS

Above: **The 8th Air Force in action. Fortresses, with contrails streaming, over Germany on their way to attack the port of Bremen, 20 December 1943.**

constantly their tactical formations in order to keep abreast of the state of the air battle. The tactical deployment at any one time had to be a compromise between various conflicting considerations – the ease and safety of flying individual aircraft, the need to concentrate defensive firepower and the desire to achieve the most accurate bombing possible. There was never a 'final answer' to the tactical problem posed but throughout the war the Americans showed considerable flexibility, ingenuity and enterprise in adapting tactics to meet prevailing conditions. But the fact remained that losses were not curbed; rather they increased with alarming rapidity, and bombing accuracy was never achieved until conditions of overwhelming air superiority had been achieved. This, of course was not achieved by the bombers but by the fighter escorts in the course of late 1943 and early 1944.

The pioneer of many of the tactical changes incorporated by the 8th Air Force was the first commander of the 305th BG, Colonel Curtis LeMay. To assert that he was actually liked by his men is to misunderstand the situation. He was respected and feared and his crews were devoted to him, but he was never liked and he won regard through his example, bravery and sheer ability. He was dubbed 'Iron-Ass,' by his men and went on to command the whole of the bomber division and then an entire Air Force in the latter stages of the Pacific War. It was under LeMay's constant probing that changes were made and improvements worked into American bombing technique.

When the 8th Air Force entered the fray its basic formation was a six-bomber squadron. Squadrons had a nominal strength of twelve, but operationally to have six available was normal. The six aircraft flew in two Vees, staggered both in height and depth. The leading aircraft in the center of the two inverted Vees were below and the two outer aircraft above the leaders. The height variation between the aircraft was about 150ft. The two flank squadrons were four miles apart and were $1\frac{1}{2}$ miles behind and about 1000ft below the lead squadron. The rear was brought up by a fourth squadron, $1\frac{1}{2}$ miles and 2000ft above the echeloned squadrons. This squadron, though above the leader, was directly in its wake.

The Vee formation had much to recommend it. It was very easy to form up. Some of the later arrangements could take more than an hour to assemble – thus cutting down range – but this one was very simple. It was also relatively easy to fly in this formation because it was not particularly demanding on attention; aircraft were spaced on a minimal lateral distance of about seventy yards. The weakness of the formation very quickly became obvious. The six-bomber formation lacked the defensive firepower needed to deter German fighters while the staggering of 24 aircraft over so much sky left them all vulnerable and unable to give one another mutual support.

The answer was to bring units closer together and in September 1942 the Americans began to experiment with a two squadron formation, both squadrons carrying nine aircraft. Squadrons incorporated three Vees, each of three bombers, with the lead squadron some 500ft below the trailing squadron which was echeloned toward the sun. All aircraft in a squadron flew at the same altitude, there being no staggering of heights within individual squadrons. This arrangement, again, had its strengths and weaknesses. Though naturally the frontage was widened and firepower was more concentrated, but only at the cost of imposing a rather inflexible linear deployment on the whole formation that made it difficult for the outer aircraft to respond to a turn. There was a tendency for the outer aircraft to lose touch and straggle, thereby falling easy victims to lurking fighters. In addition, the linear same-altitude deployment did rob the new formation of one of the advantages of staggered formation. Though Veed, the linear deployment closed down many arcs of fire and actually reduced the mutual support the bombers could afford one another.

As a result of this consideration even before the year turned the Americans again recast their tactical doctrine – under LeMay's promptings. This time they produced an eighteen-aircraft formation, stacked toward the sun, with the lead aircraft in the center. This was a considerable improvement because it allowed all the B-17s to unmask their fields of fire. The staggering and stacking of bombers, however, had certain drawbacks. These mainly arose because the Americans used successive formations in waves. Individually echeloned $1\frac{1}{2}$ miles apart, these groups incorporated the same 900ft height-differential within the lead group, but at ever-rising altitudes. In a four formation grouping this meant that the lowest aircraft in the lead formation was 4000ft lower than the trailing aircraft in the high formation. This 'Javelin' therefore encountered the difficulty of speed-differential caused by altitude-variation within and between formations. The $1\frac{1}{2}$ miles between formations, conceived in order to deny the German fighters the chance to take the optimum line of attack from dead ahead, tended to widen, thus defeating the whole purpose of the arrangement. With the higher aircraft prone to straggling, it quickly became obvious that the Javelin had to be abandoned and that a greater concentration of aircraft and firepower had to be achieved. The main problems in attempting this, however, were that tighter formation-flying imposed additional stress on crews, threatened to resurrect the old problem of masked fields of fire and increased the very real danger of bombers unloading their payloads on their low-altitude colleagues. A partial answer was provided with the 'Wedge,' introduced in February 1943. This kept the basic group formation, with the same distance between formations as with the Javelin, but instead of formations being stacked at progressively higher altitudes behind the leader, the trailing formations were deployed in echelon above and in echelon below the leader. This cut down straggling because of speed/altitude variations, but of course it could not eliminate it.

***Below:* The 15th Air Force in action. One of the very first losses suffered by the 483rd BG in April 1944 over Nis, Yugoslavia. No crewmen survived.**

***Above:* A B-17, years after the war. The crews personalized their planes, painting on names, emblems and also the number of aircraft downed.**

The problem of the Wedge was that it was inadequate to meet the challenge of the Luftwaffe, then being redeployed to the west and being concentrated in order to defend German cities. With Allied fighters unable to reach Germany the Americans had to devise a 54-bomber combat wing in March 1943 in order to try to hold off the German fighters. The Combat Wing kept the eighteen-strong formation, three formations being concentrated in a very compact unit. The wing was almost an extended skirmishing line because it envisaged one formation in the center leading and two formations slightly but clearly trailing, one above and one below the leader. This meant that the wing was concentrated within a frontage of $1\frac{1}{4}$ miles with an altitude variation of little more than $\frac{1}{2}$ mile. Critically, however, the distance between lead and trail aircraft was cut to a mere 600 yards. Here, indeed, was massive concentration of defensive firepower. By drawing in squadrons and formations into one small compact whole, the Wing could be sealed off hermetically by the firepower of over 550 machine guns. Wings were supposed to fly at six-mile intervals, but in fact this organization barely flew at all.

In April 'The Tucked-in Combat Wing' was introduced. The extent of the tuck-in can be gauged by the fact that the new formation occupied 26.5 percent of the airspace filled by the original (950 yards × 425 yards × 2900ft compared to 2340 yards × 600 yards × 2900ft). This phenomenal concentration was made possible by bringing in the trailing high and low formations almost to the point where they overlapped the leader. Within formations the three-aircraft Vees were stacked in one direction; the elements and squadrons were stacked in the opposite direction. It was by such measures that an incredible degree of compression was achieved, and it was with this bristling formation that the bombers of the 8th Air Force, spearheaded by the B-17Fs and B-17Gs, embarked upon their deep-penetration raids over Germany.

This, then, was the formation used by the 8th for most of 1943 in its attempt to make the strategic bombing philosophy work. By using such a grouping of aircraft the 8th anticipated the bombers being able to fight their way to their objectives and at the same time meet the challenge of the Luftwaffe. This attempt failed, at a devastating cost. American bomber losses in 1943 reached awesome proportions. Subsequently such losses were to be sustained only by the 492nd BG which in a three-month tour in 1944 lost what was effectively the whole of its initial establishment. Such losses in 1944 were uncommon; in 1943 they were the general rule. The Bremen raid of 17 April resulted in the destruction of or severe damage to sixty of the 115 bombers thrown against the city – over Kiel on 13 June 22 bombers were lost out of sixty. Nine days later

Top Left: **A Fortress goes down over Delmenhorst.**
Top Right: **A Fortress on Purple Heart Corner passes a stricken colleague over Stuttgart, 6 September 1943.**
Main picture: **B-17Fs in the foreground; in the distance successive units in a Combat Wing. The contrails show where previous wings have flown. In the center is a dangerously vulnerable straggler.**

Above: **LeMay's concept of 'pattern bombing' by staggered Vees. In this photograph six of the eight B-17s can be seen delivering their bomb loads.**

over Huls only sixteen bombers were lost out of 363, but no less than 170 of the survivors incurred various degrees of damage. In 'Blitz-Week' (24–30 July) the Americans lost or had to write off 100 aircraft. Ninety complete crews were lost. This represented the loss of two complete groups at a time when only fifteen had been brought up to full battle-worthiness. On the Rouen anniversary the Americans attacked Schweinfurt and Regensburg, deep in southern Germany. Of the 363 Fortresses committed sixty were destroyed – and many others written off – in the most costly raid of the war to date for the 8th. Losses were almost as heavy over Stuttgart on 6 September when fifty bombers were lost out of 388, hardly any of which found Stuttgart at all. An attempt to renew the assault on Schweinfurt in October cost the Americans 77 aircraft lost and a further 133 damaged out of a total 291 Fortresses dispatched on the mission.

By this time losses were running at nearly ten percent per mission and it was not uncommon for squadrons flying 'Purple Heart Corner' – the lowest and most exposed position in the Wing – to suffer not decimation but annihilation. The total loss of squadrons flying this vulnerable station was not unknown, and squadrons had to be rotated through this position because there was an understandable reluctance to volunteer for this station. By mid and late 1943 many groups were in a state of extremely bad demoralization as a result of their losses. Indeed, after the second Schweinfurt bombing operations had to be temporarily halted. With losses three times heavier than could be tolerated there had to be a respite. That respite, however, was tacit recognition that the bomber, despite the bravery of its crew, could not do all that was being asked of it.

Certainly the bombers had often achieved considerable successes. Many targets were badly damaged and even crippled by attacks that owed much of their effectiveness to LeMay's insistence that in formation all bombers had to bomb together. This he had advocated almost at the outset of operations, being convinced that 'pattern bombing' would be far more effective than individual bombing runs. When it came to the 1943 massed formations individual bombing runs, with aircraft jockeying for position, was out of the question. But in late 1942 LeMay and the 305th were encouraged to coordinate bombing by making all bombers drop on the signal of the leader. LeMay reasoned that while there was the possibility of all bombs being wasted as a result of error on the part of the lead bombardier, the probability was that more bombs would straddle and saturate the objective if they were dropped on the orders of the best, most highly trained and battle-experienced crew available. In this way even the weakest crew could be carried effectively. LeMay's concepts became standard operational procedure in the 8th, but that did not alter the fact that by late 1943 losses were too heavy to justify the results obtained. In 1943 the German fighters, warned by radar and deployed in depth across their homeland, could strike the heavily loaded bombers out of the skies faster than crews could be replaced.

This crisis for the American strategic offensive was overcome rapidly and in dramatic fashion in the same way fortune changed sides between March and May 1943 in the Battle of the Atlantic. In October 1943 the Fortresses (and Liberators) found they could not withstand concentrated attacks by the main-line German fighters, the FW190 and the Me109G. Soon after the tide turned for the Americans. The combination of three fighters – a much improved P-47 Thunderbolt, the P-38 twin-boomed Lightning and the P-51 Mustang – began to drive the Luftwaffe out of the skies. The most important of these aircraft was the Mustang, a fighter whose range allowed it to operate east of the Oder-Neisse. With a range of 1500 miles and a top speed of 440mph, it could outpace both the FW190 and Me109G with ease, and it could out-dive and out-turn both German aircraft. Only in rate of roll could the German aircraft compete on anything like equal terms. In the P-51 the Americans had a fighter of superb quality, and Spaatz and his fighter commander, Kepner, knew how to use it. With the strategic bombing campaign having failed, Spaatz was determined to keep the bombers in the air to force the Germans to give battle to the Mustang on unequal terms. Rather than being the means of winning air superiority through bombing, the bombers were made the means by which an air supremacy battle could be provoked and won. Kepner used his fighters not simply as escorts but as fighting patrols to seek out enemy fighters throughout the length of Germany. This did not mean that bomber losses dropped immediately. As the battle for supremacy intensified bomber losses were heavy. Over Berlin on 6 March 1944, 72 bombers were lost and 102 more received serious damage out of a total number of 730. The 350th BS lost ten of its number in this raid.

The emergence of the Mustang necessitated another tactical change for the bombers. Formations were reduced to three squadrons of twelve aircraft, with the lead squadron in the center. The lead squadron, or individual aircraft in it, were given the relatively few air-to-ground radars available in early 1944 (H2S to the British, known as H2X to the Americans). The trail squadrons formed up above and below. Cut in strength by a third, this formation occupied seventeen percent more airspace than the previous system, but was easier for the bombers to fly and the Mustangs to escort. This formation proved very effective for the best part of a year. Occasionally major efforts by the Luftwaffe, including the first use of jet attacks, were costly, but with the ebbing strength of the Luftwaffe the bombers' main threat came from ever more powerful flak defenses in the last eighteen months of the war. The problem for the bombers was simple. The Germans could deduce the bombers' probable line of approach to their objective and concentrate on that line a massive volume of fire through which the bombers had to fly in order to reach the target. To improve their chances of survival, in 1945 the Americans opened up their formations to try to confuse the German flak gunners. The bombers were deployed over a greater depth of sky (1150ft) than ever before with four nine-strong squadrons in formation. One high and one low squadron flanked the leader who was trailed by a still lower rear squadron. This formation occupied 43 percent more airspace than its predecessor, making it harder for the flak to assess altitude correctly and to shift fire with rapidity and accuracy. It was this tactical formation that saw out the end of the war.

Below: **Major General William Kepner (left) with Lieutenant General Carl Spaatz.**

Such were the tactics employed by the bombers of the 8th Air Force. The chart on page 61 clearly shows the buildup of the 8th in the course of the war. Eaker, in his earliest demands, assessed the heavy bomber needs to be 944 by 1 July 1943, 1192 by 1 October and 2702 by 1 April 1944. In fact these target figures were very nearly met at every stage, but the chart shows clearly that of the 42 groups that at various times served with the 8th (the 482nd being discounted), no less than nineteen entered combat after 30 November 1944. This was when only 21 of the once 23 heavy groups remained with the 8th Air Force. In the early months of 1944 the strength of the 8th almost doubled. The sad fact of this from the B-17s viewpoint was that whereas only four groups were equipped with B-17s, those that remained had B-24s. In the autumn, however, five groups, the 34th, 486th, 487th, 490th and 493rd converted to B-17Gs, and 72 percent of these groups' missions were flown in the Fortress. It was as a result of the massive build-up of B-24s in early 1944 that there was an almost equal balance between B-17s and B-24s in the 8th in June 1944. In that month 49.77 percent of the first line heavy bombers were B-24s; in July 48.70 percent. Both before and after that time, however, the overwhelming balance was in favor of the B-17. The B-24 build-up was mainly directed toward the invasion.

The total number of American strategic bombers available to the Supreme Allied Commander (General Dwight D Eisenhower) on any day in September was 4202. This is the strength on which the Supreme Commander could call. In fact the total number of heavy bombers within the 8th and 15th was at least 25 percent more than his paper allocation, but the extra numbers were not first-line aircraft and includes replacement, training and assorted aircraft. The total available with RAF Bomber Command was 6073. Of this final total 76 percent were operational at any one time.

Excluding the RAF and the US 15th Air Force, certain calculations may be made regarding the B-17 and the 8th Air Force. In the whole of the war the 8th flew 10,802 missions of which 6945 (64.29 percent) were flown by B-17s. Liberators flew a total of 3706 missions (34.31 percent). From the chart it can be seen that 4255 heavy bombers were listed as Missing in Action, and an unknown number were written off. Roger Freeman in *The US Strategic Bomber* (MacDonald and Jane's, London, 1975) gives the losses of the 8th as 5548 heavy bombers from all causes during combat. Of this total German aircraft are credited with 44.20 percent and flak with 43.96 percent. There seems to be no complete total of heavy bombers lost outside of combat. With incomplete data, drawn from just 27 groups there were at least 864 bombers classified as 'Other Operational Losses.' Of these totals it would seem that at least 75 percent of the losses were sustained by the Fortresses because losses equipped only with the B-24 totalled 944, while 290 aircraft were lost from the five 'mixed' groups. What this meant in human or in Group terms can be seen by a reference to the career of the 388th, the Group selected for the Castor experiments. Its total operational losses were 179 aircraft with an additional 34 written off as a result of accidents and other causes. Only 270 aircraft served with the Group, which means that in addition to losing between four and five times its original strength, the group lost 78.89 percent of its total effective strength in the course of its operations. One hundred and thirty five of its 450 crews were listed as Missing in Action. In two years of combat some ground crews serviced as many as eight different aircraft, seventy airmen having passed by in that time. Only two aircraft of the original batch were still in service at the end of the war, and not that many more of the original crewmen. Such was the price of victory.

APPENDICES

1. Deployment of B-17 Flying Fortresses, other than those with 8th Air Force

Metropolitan Homeland, USA

Number of Groups: 21.
(Bombardment: 18. Search Attack: 1. Reconnaissance: 1. Bombardment/Search Attack: 1.)
Bombardment Groups (with squadrons):

6th (3/25/74/395/397)	346th (502/503/504/505)
29th (6/29/52)	383rd (540/541/542/543)
34th (4/7/18/391)	393rd (580/581/582/583)
39th (6/61/62)	395th (588/589/590/591)
40th (29/44/45/74)	396th (592/593/594/595)
88th (316/317/318/399)	444th (676/677/678/679)
304th (361/362/363/421)	469th (796/797/798/799)
331st (461/462/463/464)	504th (393/398/421/507)
333rd (466/467/468/469)	505th (482/483/484/485)

Nominal squadron strength: 71
Actual squadron strength: 70 (29th BS in two Groups)

Reconnaissance Group: 9th No squadrons permanently attached.
Search-Attack Group: 1st Three squadrons attached: 2nd, 3rd and 4th.
Dual-Role Group: 9th Four squadrons attached: 1st, 5th, 99th and 430th.

Pacific Theater of Operations

Number of Groups: 5.
(Bombardment: 4. Reconnaissance: 1.)
Bombardment Groups (with squadrons):

4th (23/31/72/394)	19th (14/28/30/40/93)
11th (26/42/98/431)	43rd (63/64/65/403)

Nominal squadron strength: 17.
Reconnaissance Group: 11th. Three squadrons attached: 1st, 3rd and 19th.

PTO/China-Burma-India Theater

Total strength was the 7th Bombardment Group with four squadrons, the 9th, 11th, 22nd and 88th attached.

The MTO/ETO

In the course of the war various US Air Forces served in the Mediterranean area, with groups and squadrons being 'borrowed' almost as standard practice between forces. This makes giving an account of units in the area extremely complicated, but it is probably easiest to account for B-17 participation in the MTO/ETO with reference to the 15th Air Force.

Formed from various forces in the Mediterranean, the 15th operated a total of 21 Bombardment Groups. Of this total six were equipped with B-17s. These were the

2nd (20/49/96/429) Entered service 28 April 1943 with 2nd Air Force.
97th (340/341/342/414) Entered service 17 August 1942 with 8th Air Force.
99th (346/347/348/416) Entered service 31 March 1943.
301st (32/352/353/419) Entered service 5 September 1942 with 8th Air Force.
463rd (772/773/774/775) Entered service 16 March 1944.
483rd (815/816/817/818) Entered service 12 April 1944.

All these groups were allocated to the 5th Bombardment Wing, one of six operated by 15th Air Force.

Until the end of 1943 there were more B-17s than B-24s with the 15th, but thereafter the massive build-up of B-24 strength clearly relegated the B-17 to second place. By June 1944 less than one in four heavy bombers was a B-17, though this imbalance was 'corrected' slightly before the end of the war as a result of the decline in overall numbers of Liberators on station and the expansion of the numbers of Fortresses. By May 1945 B-17s formed nearly forty percent of the total first line bomber strength available to the 15th Air Force.

Total losses among the Bombardment Groups is given by Freeman as 2519. With no breakdown available one can make no comment other than that the vast majority of these losses must have been sustained by the B-24s.

In addition to the Bombardment Groups two B-17 equipped Reconnaissance Groups served in the Mediterranean. These were:
5th (21/22/23/24) and 68th (16/111/122/125/127/154).
The 3rd Photographic Group, containing one squadron with B-17s, also served in the Mediterranean.

Note:
One Bombardment Group, the 34th, appears in two lists: the Metropolitan Homeland and the 8th Air Force. For most of the war it was in the USA where it served as the training cadre for the 8th Air Force. It was activated for war in early 1944.

Below: **One of the very last B-17s, one of batch B-17G-100-VE. Too late to see service, she was used in radio-controlled flight tests and at Bikini.**

2. Nominal Role of the Bombardment Groups that served with the 8th Air Force in Britain

Group:	sqn:	sqn:	sqn:	sqn:	ttl;	.ac.	.ac.	1942 JJASOND: 1943 JFMAMJJASOND: 1944 JFMAMJJASOND: 1945 JFMA	Missions	Sorties	Payload in tons	MIA	OOL
34th	4	7	18	391	4	G	24	M————	108/170	5,713	13,425	34	39
44th					4		24	N————	343	8,009	18,980	153	39
91st	322	323	324	401	4	F	G	N————	340/340	9,591	22,142	197	?
92nd	325	326	327	407	4	F	G	S————	308/308	8,633	20,829	154	?
93rd					4		24	O————	396	8,169	19,004	100	40
94th	331	332	333	410	4	F	G	M————	324/324	8,884	18,925	153	27
95th	334	335	336	412	4	F	G	M————	320/320	8,903	19,769	157	39
96th	337	338	339	413	4	F	G	M————	321/321	8,924	19,277	189	50
97th	340	341	342	414	4	E	F	A–O	14/ 14	247	395	4	?
100th	349	350	351	418	4	F	G	J————	306/306	8,630	19,257	177	52
301st	32	352	353	419	4	F		S–N	8/ 8	104	186	1	?
303rd	358	359	360	427	4	F	G	N————	364/364	10,721	24,918	165	?
305th	364	365	366	422	4	F	G	N————	337/337	9,231	22,363	154	?
306th	367	368	369	423	4	F	G	O————	342/342	9,614	22,575	171	?
322nd					4		26	M—O	34	?	?	12	?
323rd					4		26	J—O	33	?	?	3	?
351st	508	509	510	511	4	F	G	M————	311/311	8,600	20,357	124	?
379th	524	525	526	527	4	F	G	M————	330/330	10,492	26,460	141	?
381st	532	533	534	535	4	F	G	J————	296/296	9,035	22,160	131	?
384th	544	545	546	547	4	F	G	J————	314/314	9,348	22,415	159	?
385th	548	549	550	551	4	F	G	J————	296/296	8,264	18,494	129	40
386th					4		26	J—O	30	?	?	6	?
387th					4		26	A—O	29	?	?	2	?
388th	560	561	562	563	4	F	G						
						24	34	J————	306/331	8,051	18,162	142	37
389th					4		24	J————	321	7,579	17,548	116	37
390th	568	569	570	571	4	F	G	A————	300/300	8,725	19,059	144	32
392nd					4		24	S————	285	7,060	17,452	127	57
398th	600	601	602	603	4	G		M————	195/195	6,419	15,781	58	?
401st	612	613	614	615	4	G		N————	255/255	7,430	17,778	95	?
445th					4		24	D————	282	7,145	16,732	108	25
446th					4		24	D————	273	7,259	16,819	58	28
447th	708	709	710	711	4	G		D————	257/257	7,605	17,103	153	27
448th					4		24	D————	262	6,774	15,272	101	34
452nd	728	729	730	731	4	G		F————	250/250	7,279	16,467	110	48
453rd					4		24	F————	259	6,655	15,804	58	?
457th	748	749	750	751	4	G		F————	237/237	7,086	16,916	83	?
458th					4		24	F————	240	5,759	13,204	47	18
466th					4		24	M————	232	5,762	12,914	47	24
467th					4		24	A————	212	5,538	13,333	29	19
482nd	812	813	814		3	F/G	24	S————	?	?	?	7	?*
486th	832	833	834	835	4	G	24	M————	142/188	6,173	14,517	33	24
487th	836	837	838	839	4	G	24	M————	139/185	6,021	14,041	33	24
489th					4		24	M—N	106	2,998	6,951	29	12
490th	848	849	850	851	4	G	24	M————	118/158	5,060	12,407	22	32
491st					4		24	J————	187	5,005	12,304	47	23
492nd					4		24	M–A	64	1,513	3,757	51	6
493rd	860	861	862	863	4	G	24	J————	110/157	4,871	12,188	41	31

Key:

- sqn — squadron number
- ttl — total squadrons in group
- ac — type of aircraft used: letters refer to Mark of B-17 and numbers to other types of bomber
- MIA — aircraft missing in action
- OOL — other operational losses
- ? — Information unavailable

Letters in date list give month of first operational mission by group or part of group and, where appropriate, when left 8AF

Missions: first figure is B-17 total
second figure total all aircraft

*Unit raised in UK. Used in radio, radar and pathfinder tasks.

Others:

5th Emergency Rescue Squadron: used B-17Gs after Mar 45.

15th Photographic Squadron: One of five squadrons; only one to use B-17F. Part of 3rd PG. Assigned to but not active with 8AF.

422nd BS (renumbered 858th then 406th) Night Leaflet Squadron. B-17F/G from Sep 43 until Aug 44.

652nd BS One of four squadron, part of 25th BG (Recce). Only squadron with B-17Gs; after Nov 44.

803rd BS (renumbered 36th) Formed Jan 44 as ECM unit. Used B-17F/G after Jun 44.

3. Specifications of the B-17 Flying Fortress

Model	299	Y1B-17	Y1B-17A	B-17B	B-17C	B-17D	B17E	B-17F
Engine	R-1690-E	R-1820-39	R-1820-51	R-1820-51	R-1820-65	R-1820-65	R-1820-65	R-1820-97
Orthodox hp	750	930	1,000	1,000	1,200	1,200	1,200	1,200
Span	103ft 9in	103ft 9in	103ft 9in	103ft 9in	103ft 9in	103ft 9in	103ft 9in	103ft 9in
Length	61ft 10in	68ft 4in	68ft 4in	67ft 11in	67ft 11in	67ft 11in	73ft 10in	74ft 9in
Empty Weight	21,657lb	24,460lb	31,160lb	27,650lb	30,600lb	30,960lb	32,250lb	34,000lb
Maximum Weight	43,000lb	43,650lb	45,650lb	48,000lb	49,650lb	49,650lb	54,000lb	65,500lb
Maximum Speed	236mph	256mph	295mph	292mph	323mph*	318mph	317mph	299mph
Service Ceiling	24,600ft	30,000ft	38,000ft	38,000ft	37,000ft	37,000ft	36,500ft	37,500ft
Rate of climb	6mins to 10,000ft	6mins 30sec to 10,000ft	7mins 48sec to 10,000ft	7mins to 10,000ft	7mins 30sec to 10,000ft	7mins 12sec to 10,000ft	7mins 6sec to 10,000ft	25mins 42sec to 20,000ft
Normal Range	2,400 miles	2,400 miles	2,400 miles	2,400 miles	2,000 miles	2,000 miles	2,000 miles	1,300 or 2,200 miles
Maximum Range	3,000 miles	3,400 miles	3,600 miles	3,600 miles	3,400 miles	3,400 miles	3,200 miles	2,680 or 3,800 miles
Normal bomb load	4,000lb	4,000lb	4,000lb	4,000lb	4,000lb	4,000lb	4,000lb	4,000lb
Normal maximum bomb load	4,000lb	8,000lb	8,000lb	8,000lb	4,000lb	4,000lb	4,000lb	13,600lb
Crew members	6	6	6	6	6	6	10	10
Defensive Firepower	Five .3	One .3 Six .5	One .3 Six .5	One .3 Six .5	One .3 Six .5	One .3 Six .5	One .3 Eight .5	Eleven .5

*The speed given for the B-17C takes no account of the speed of 353mph achieved by a B-17C of the Royal Air Force. All characteristics listed are liable to dispute because there are as many 'maximum speeds' as there are sources. Much depends on the state of an aircraft, climatic conditions etc, in any giving of weights, speeds etc. The list given is an attempt to collate various information, but the basis for this material is Roger A Freeman's *American Bombers of World War Two*.

4. Construction of B-17s

Prototypes and early Marks

229	1	No military serial number Registration number NX-13372
Y1B-17	13	36-149ff
Y1B-17A	1	37-369
B-17B	39	38-211 to 38-223 38-258 to 38-270 38-583 to 38-584 38-610 39-1 to 39-10
B-17C	38	40-2042 to 40-2079
B-17D	42	40-3059 to 40-3100
B-17E	512	41-2393 to 41-2669 41-9011 to 41-9245

In the subsequent lists, the construction per company (Boeing, Douglas and Vega) is shown with Batch Number, full designation and military serial numbers. All aircraft in a given batch are numbered consecutively unless otherwise stated.

B-17F

B-17F- 1-BO	50	41-24340ff	B-17F- 1-DL	3	42- 2964ff
B-17F- 5-BO	50	41-24390ff	B-17F- 5-DL	12	42- 2967ff
B-17F- 10-BO	50	41-24440ff	B-17F- 10-DL	25	42- 2979ff
B-17F- 15-BO	14	41-24490ff	B-17F- 15-DL	35	42- 3004ff
B-17F- 20-BO	36	41-24504ff	B-17F- 20-DL	35	42- 3039ff
B-17F- 25-BO	45	41-24540ff	B-17F- 25-DL	75	42- 3074ff
B-17F- 27-BO	55	41-24585ff	B-17F- 30-DL	40	42- 3149ff
B-17F- 30-BO	29	42- 5050ff	B-17F- 35-DL	40	42- 3189ff
B-17F- 35-BO	71	42- 5079ff	B-17F- 40-DL	55	42- 3229ff
B-17F- 40-BO	100	42- 5150ff	B-17F- 45-DL	55	42- 3284ff
B-17F- 45-BO	100	42- 5250ff	B-17F- 50-DL	55	42- 3339ff
B-17F- 50-BO	135	42- 5350ff	B-17F- 55-DL	29	42- 3394ff
B-17F- 55-BO	65	42-29467ff	B-17F- 60-DL	26	42- 3423ff
B-17F- 60-BO	100	42-29532ff	B-17F- 65-DL	34	42- 3449ff
B-17F- 65-BO	100	42-29632ff	B-17F- 70-DL	21	42- 3483ff
B-17F- 70-BO	100	42-29732ff	B-17F- 75-DL	59	42- 3504ff
B-17F- 75-BO	100	42-29832ff	B-17F- 80-DL	6	42-37714ff
B-17F- 80-BO	100	42-29932ff	B-17F- 1-VE	5	42- 5705ff
B-17F- 85-BO	100	42-30032ff	B-17F- 5-VE	15	42- 5710ff
B-17F- 90-BO	100	42-30132ff	B-17F- 10-VE	20	42- 5725ff
B-17F- 95-BO	100	42-30232ff	B-17F- 15-VE	20	42- 5745ff
B-17F-100-BO	100	42-30332ff	B-17F- 20-VE	40	42- 5765ff
B-17F-105-BO	100	42-30432ff	B-17F- 25-VE	50	42- 5805ff
B-17F-110-BO	85	42-30532ff	B-17F- 30-VE	50	42- 5855ff
B-17F-115-BO	115	42-30617ff	B-17F- 35-VE	50	42- 5905ff
B-17F-120-BO	100	42-30732ff	B-17F- 40-VE	75	42- 5955ff
B-17F-125-BO	100	42-30832ff	B-17F- 45-VE	75	42- 6030ff
B-17F-130-BO	100	42-30932ff	B-17F- 50-VE	100	42- 6105ff

Production:	Boeing	2,300
	Douglas	605
	Vega	500
		3,405

B-17G

B-17G- 1-BO	100	42- 31032ff	B-17G- 50-DL	250	44- 6251ff
B-17G- 5-BO	100	42- 31132ff	B-17G- 55-DL	125	44- 6501ff
B-17G- 10-BO	100	42- 31232ff	B-17G- 60-DL	125	44- 6626ff
B-17G- 15-BO	100	42- 31332ff	B-17G- 65-DL	125	44- 6751ff
B-17G- 20-BO	200	42- 31432ff	B-17G- 70-DL	125	44- 6876ff
B-17G- 25-BO	100	42- 31632ff	B-17G- 75-DL	125	44- 83236ff
B-17G- 30-BO	200	42- 31732ff	B-17G- 80-DL	125	44- 83361ff
B-17G- 35-BO	185	42- 31932ff	B-17G- 85-DL	100	44- 83486ff
B-17G- 40-BO	115	42- 97058ff	B-17G- 90-DL	100	44- 83586ff
B-17G- 45-BO	235	42- 97173ff	B-17G- 95-DL	200	44- 83686ff
B-17G- 50-BO	165	42-102379ff	B-17G- 1-VE	100	42- 39758ff
B-17G- 55-BO	200	42-102544ff	B-17G- 5-VE	100	42- 39858ff
B-17G- 60-BO	235	42-102744ff	B-17G- 10-VE	100	42- 39958ff
B-17G- 65-BO	165	43- 37509ff	B-17G- 15-VE	100	42- 97436ff
B-17G- 70-BO	200	43- 37674ff	B-17G- 20-VE	100	42- 97536ff
B-17G- 75-BO	200	43- 37874ff	B-17G- 25-VE	100	42- 97636ff
B-17G- 80-BO	200	43- 38074ff	B-17G- 30-VE	100	42- 97736ff
B-17G- 85-BO	200	43- 38274ff	B-17G- 35-VE	100	42- 97836ff
B-17G- 90-BO	200	43- 38474ff	B-17G- 40-VE	100	42- 97936ff
B-17G- 95-BO	200	43- 38674ff	B-17G- 45-VE	100	44- 8001ff
B-17G-100-BO	200	43- 38874ff	B-17G- 50-VE	100	44- 8101ff
B-17G-105-BO	200	43- 39074ff	B-17G- 55-VE	100	44- 8201ff
B-17G-110-BO	200	43- 39274ff	B-17G- 60-VE	100	44- 8301ff
B-17G- 5-DL	1	42- 3563	B-17G- 65-VE	100	44- 8401ff
B-17G- 10-DL	84	see note	B-17G- 70-VE	100	44- 8501ff
B-17G- 15-DL	90	42- 37804ff	B-17G- 75-VE	100	44- 8601ff
B-17G- 20-DL	95	42- 37894ff	B-17G- 80-VE	100	44- 8701ff
B-17G- 25-DL	95	42- 37989ff	B-17G- 85-VE	100	44- 8801ff
B-17G- 30-DL	130	42- 38084ff	B-17G- 90-VE	100	44- 8901ff
B-17G- 35-DL	250	42-106984ff	B-17G- 95-VE	100	44- 85492ff
B-17G- 40-DL	125	44- 6001ff	B-17G-100-VE	100	44- 85592ff
B-17G- 45-DL	125	44- 6126ff	B-17G-105-VE	100	44- 85692ff
			B-17G-110-VE	50	44- 85792ff

Production:	Boeing	4,035
	Douglas	2,395
	Vega	2,250
		8,680

Note: The 84 production models of B-17G- 10-DL given serial numbers 42-37716 and 42-37721ff.

Summary of Construction

Model	Orders	Boeing	Douglas	Vega
229	1	1		
Y1B-17	1	13		
Y1B-17A	1	1		
B-17B	1	39		
B-17C	1	38		
B-17D	1	42		
B-17E	1	512		
B-17F	56	2,300	605	500
B-17G	65	4,035	2,395	2,250
		6,981 (54.83%)	3,000 (23.56%)	2,750 (21.60%)

Total production: 12,761.

Left: **A B-17E in service with RAF Coastal Command, 1945. Many later B-17s with the RAF were used in airborne radar navigation and ECM roles.**

Acknowledgments

Most of the photographs were supplied by the Taylor Picture Library. The author would like to thank the Boeing Company for allowing us to reproduce them, and also

Warren Bodie: p 60.
Charles Brown: pp 20–21.
Imperial War Museum: pp 51, 59.
Lockheed: pp 22 (bottom), 29 (bottom both), 31 (top).
McDonnell Douglas: pp 10–11, 12–13, 29 (top).
National Archives: p 10 (bottom left).
Michael Ross: p 62.
Bob Snyder: p 33 (bottom and center)
Gordon Williams: pp 42–43.
USAF: pp 11 (bottom right), 27 (top), 34 (top), 35 (top), 36–37, 38, 39, 41 (top), 44–45 (bottom all four), 46, 47, 48, 49 (top), 52, 53, 54, 55, 56, 57.
US Army: pp 14–15, 19 (top).

Artwork

Mike Badrocke: Cutaway on pp 34–35, line drawings on p 37.
Mike Bailey: Cover sideview.
Mike Trim: Sideview on pp 36–37.

Below: **B-17s of the 390th Bomb Group, 13th Bomb Wing of the US 8th AF on a mission over Germany. Note the vapor trails from the escorting P-47s.**